# POLICE DOGS ARE FUN!

## *The Story of Police Dog Triton*

Steve Lewis

Parts of the book were originally published under the title
'Triton: A Police Dog's Tale' by the Police Review Publishing Company,
London E14 9FZ

My grateful thanks to Ann Campbell of Abergynolwyn for her invaluable
help in republishing this book in 2005 and to Paul and Peggy McGregor
for their assistance in the 2009 reprint.

A donation to charity will be made from the sale of each book from the
2009 edition

# CHAPTER ONE

## *CHARLIE MEETS TRITON*

'Go on son, get the bastard,' was not, I reflected afterwards, exactly a command straight out of the Home Office Manual of Guidance in the Training and Care of Police Dogs. As a command, however, it seemed remarkably effective as Triton shot off into the darkness across the waste ground of a demolition site.

In spite of the fact that there was a large dog chasing a man through piles of rubble, there wasn't a sound to be heard, except the red-hot engine of the police dog van ticking and burping as it thankfully cooled down after the usual hair-raising race round the back streets.

The initial call on this incident from the Control Room had been routine. A Traffic car had stopped a suspect vehicle with two men on board and I had been sent as a precaution in case things went wrong. Things went wrong when I was about half-way there. The passenger had caused no trouble, but when the driver had been asked to open the boot of the car, he had grabbed a wheelbrace and without warning had crashed it over the head of my colleague, Terry, fracturing his skull.

As Terry collapsed, the man took his chance and evading a despairing dive from Terry's observer had sprinted off up the road, vaulted over a wall and was lost to sight.

These events had been related to me by the Control Room as I was on the way to the incident and I endeavoured to coax an extra few miles per hour from the already screaming mini-van. In between answering the radio, changing gear, trying to steer and looking for my torch, I was trying to calculate how far and in which direction the wanted man was likely to run in the two minutes it would take me to arrive.

I had to guess right first time. You don't get two chances very often in the city, which swallows criminals up without trace, especially if they are local lads who know their way about. I hoped this one wasn't local.

Triton wasn't helping. Like most experienced police dogs he knew that when I drove like a madman something was up, and from his cage in the back he was either voicing his approval of my efforts to get there quickly or his disapproval of being bounced around like a cat in a spin drier. Either way, as I say, he wasn't helping.

With about half a mile to go I cut the speed of the van and started looking carefully, up side streets, down alley-ways, entries anywhere. I wanted to find this one, Terry was a mate of mine. Out of the corner of my eye I caught a movement by a builder's hut, no more than a shadow altering but it was enough. I swung the van round and bounced it up the kerb so that the headlights shone across the side of the hut.

Triton saw him then as the lights picked him out, and a low rumbling growl echoed round the back of the van. As I scrambled to get out of the van, the figure disappeared into the night while I was frantically tearing myself free from the wire to the radio hand-set which had wrapped itself round my left leg. Cursing the powers that be who put six foot, fifteen stone policemen into Mini-vans, I grabbed the handle to the rear doors and wrenched them open. From then on I became surplus to requirements.

As I reached for his choke chain so I could line him up and send him off in the right direction, Triton must have decided that enough time had been wasted by my clumsiness. He ducked under my hand and simply went.

He didn't need lining up or sending in the right direction, he had seen enough and he was gone.

'Stand still,' I shouted. 'This is the police. Stand still or I'll send the dog" It was a little late, I admit, as a warning challenge but things were happening a bit quickly.

I set off after the dog, violently striking my torch with my free hand to try and make it work, but not a glimmer came. Police torches never work when you really need them, it's one of the first things you learn when you join, and where the hell had my dog got to.

As if in answer a loud bark came from over on my left, instantly followed by a man shouting. As the volume of noise increased, the barking sounded more joyful, I thought. The shouting sounded more desperate.

The barking stopped to be replaced by a growling sound rather like a puppy worrying a bone, but louder, a lot louder. The shouting continued, also a lot louder.

Trying to fend off a police dog with a wheelbrace is not a good idea, as any offer of resistance tends to annoy the dog, not that Triton needed annoying, perhaps he knew that Terry was a mate of mine.

The object of our attention, Charlie Sutton, was nineteen years of age and over six foot tall and when he had heard Triton racing up behind him, he had turned and swung the wheelbrace at the dog's head.

Unhappily for Charlie, Triton was far more experienced in dealing with violent criminals than Charlie was at dealing with ninety-three pounds of speeding Alsatian dog.

Checking slightly, Triton avoided the swinging wheelbrace and latched firmly onto Charlie's right arm with all forty-two teeth in a bone-crunching bite, knocking Charlie flat on his back.

Charlie was now very, very sorry he had started all this but, still determined, he endeavoured to kick Triton in the ribs. In a flash, Triton transferred his attention to Charlie's right leg and when I came stumbling over the rubble he was actually dragging him back towards me.

Not everybody is pleased to see a policeman, but Charlie certainly seemed relieved to see me. 'Get your frigging dog off my frigging leg,' he screamed.

'Good lad,' I said to Triton. 'What a clever boy. Leave him.' Triton looked up at me with his deep brown eyes and seemed to raise his eyebrows quizzically, as if to say 'Already? I've only just found him.'

'Leave him,' I shouted, and gradually and carefully Triton let go of Charlie's leg. Charlie subsided, moaning.

'On your feet,' I ordered, "you're nicked for wounding a policeman and anything else I can think of.'

'I can't bloody walk,' said Charlie, 'That bloody thing's crippled me.'

'Get up,' I said with an edge in my voice, reinforced by a soft growl from Triton, ever watchful for any sudden move. 'Alright, alright,' grumbled Charlie hastily, just hang onto that bastard.'

I picked up the wheelbrace and followed Charlie as he hobbled painfully back towards the dog van. He made it more difficult for himself as he would persist in turning round all the time staring malevolently at Triton.

In return Triton seemed to be grinning.

# CHAPTER TWO

## *A FLASHER CAUGHT IN THE DINGLES*

On one of those lovely sunny afternoons that you always remember I was on foot patrol, in the days when City Dog Handlers had time for foot patrol, and police dog Triton and I were at peace with the world. We were strolling along in our favourite patch of ground, the Dingles, which was a long thin park formed out of the waste land a hundred yards or so either side of the River Cole, but over a mile long.

With Triton paying his full attention to every tree and fence post I had time to contemplate the finer things in life, such as that young mother in a mini-skirt bending over her baby's pushchair. Any minute now, I thought, she is going to see Triton and ask if she can stroke him. This time I MUST NOT reply that she can stroke me as well if she likes. That didn't go down too well with the last young lady I tried it with, but you can't win them all.

My blissful reverie was interrupted by the sound of a man's voice coming from the other side of the river behind the thick screen of bushes growing on both banks.

'What do you think of that then, darlin?' boomed the voice.

The lady to whom it was addressed did not sound particularly impressed.

'Oh you filthy sod,' was all I heard as I turned to call my dog.

'Triton,' I hissed, 'Come here, good lad.'

The urgency in my voice made him look round, suddenly alert, his ears pricked, his eyes watchful.

'Come ON, I implored him, trying to shout quietly, and I started to run towards the river, clipping his lead onto his collar as I went.

Now excited, he dragged me through a hawthorn bush and down the steep three-foot high bank of the river to the water's edge. Triton charged on into the water while I desperately looked for a way across.

Now the River Cole is not exactly in the same class as the Thames or the Mersey and was only about ten feet wide and nine inches deep at the point where I was dancing about on the gravel, but I didn't want to get my feet wet. My wellies, of course, were in the dog van, but who was going to need wellies on such a fine sunny day? Well I did, but if I jumped onto that milk crate there, and then got my left foot onto that old car wheel there, I might just make it. It was Triton's over-enthusiasm that brought disaster. Just as I got my left foot onto the wheel he went lunging forward up the opposite bank, completely destroying what meagre balance I had, by jerking me violently sideways and plunging my right foot into the water.

'You stupid bastard,' I mouthed, but then forgot all about my sopping trousers as we scrambled up the far bank and burst through the nettles. The sight that greeted us was a dog handler's dream.

There was our man, trousers round his knees, still engaged in the act of lewdly and indecently exposing his person as they say or - as everybody else says - he was flashing. He was facing slightly away from me, totally engrossed in what he was doing and still trying to attract the attention of the rapidly retreating woman.

I could have walked up behind him and tapped him on the shoulder, but I looked down at Triton, saw the pleading look in his eyes, and succumbed to temptation. I always was a sucker for a pair of big brown eyes.

'Hey mate,' I shouted from about forty yards away, 'I reckon you're in a bit of trouble.'

He spun round like he had been struck by lightning and I noticed that his face wasn't the first thing that dropped. His misfortunes then multiplied one after the other. In his panic to get away he tried to do too many things at once. Instead of pulling up his trousers first and then starting to run, he got it all wrong and tried to run off while still bent double and frantically tugging at his waistband.

In between my fits of laughter at the sight of his white backside bounding across the park, I managed to gasp out 'Stand still or I'll send my dog.' And when my challenge was ignored I unclipped Triton's lead. This was not so easy as it sounds with Triton jumping about and straining forward with every muscle in his body to be off and running.

From then on it was no contest really. Triton homed in on his target like a guided missile. Although like all police dogs he was trained to bite a man's arm, that big white circle of flesh was not to be ignored, and within a few short seconds our flasher had the biggest thrill he had ever had when Triton sunk his teeth into his behind and knocked him forwards onto his head.

He was still grovelling in the grass when I came panting up to a very satisfied-looking Triton, standing over his prisoner, willing him to get up and try again.

'Oh God, what have I done,' moaned our flasher through a mouthful of grass.

'Well mate,' I said, 'it's usually called indecent exposure, and you're just about to be arrested for it.'

We then went through the 'I don't know what came over me. I've never done it before. Will it get into the papers?' routine, when the woman complainant came over to us.

'That'll teach him officer,' she said, 'filthy swine.' She paused. 'Oh, is that what he looks like? I didn't notice his face before.

It was enough to make a dog laugh.

# CHAPTER THREE

## *A HEAP OF TROUBLE*

'Any mobile near Acocks Green Village? Respond, please'. Mac's voice crackled in my personal radio.

'Dog van about two minutes away,' I replied.

'Thanks, Steve,' Mac replied. 'Bit of a disturbance outside the New Inns. Let me know if you need any assistance, we're a bit short.'

I sighed, we were always a bit short, and there was always a bit of a disturbance outside the New Inns on a Saturday night. The gearbox on the Mini-van whined and the front suspension made clonking noises as I bounded down the hill into Acocks Green Village. Not as one might suppose from its name a leafy little hamlet, but now in the early 70s, a suburb of Birmingham, overtaken by progress and transformed into a large council estate. The only remnant of the village green was now a triangle of tarmac submerged by parked cars and surrounded by double yellow lines.

As I approached this less than sylvan setting, I saw that there was indeed a crowd of people outside the New Inns, and Police Dog Triton, from his position behind me, saw them too.

Already aroused by the increased speed of the dog van, he began voicing his disapproval of the gathering. As far as Triton was concerned, any number of people more than about two was a crowd, and if it was on Saturday night, they were hostile.

Unsuccessfully commanding Triton to be quiet, I pulled my dark blue Mini-van past the pub and parked it neatly on the bus stop.

I struggled out of the van, trying for once not to knock my cap off on the roof, and surveyed the scene. Quite a few of the group had melted away as I arrived, and I was left with about a dozen youths standing round what I thought at first to be a small stranded whale.

Quickly realizing that whales neither wore trousers nor got washed up in Acocks Green very often, I took a closer look and saw that the thing I was observing was a very fat young man, about twenty years old and as many stone in weight.

I approached.

'That's Archie,' volunteered one helpful young man.

'Is it really,' I said, 'and what's Archie been doing?'

'He's had a bit to drink,' said another, unnecessarily. 'He was alright inside the boozer but he went a bit funny when he got here and then he fell in a heap.'

Heap was the word, what on earth was I going to do with him? I looked round, both for inspiration and, more helpfully, a passing mobile crane, but none came.

'Are yer going to lock him up?' said one of Archie's mates.

I shuddered. I could just imagine our Geordie office sergeant's reaction if I deposited Archie in the dock. No, life was too short for that sort of trouble. Something, however, had to be done.

'Where does he live?" I asked hopefully.

'Up by the buzz garridge,' came the reply.

My spirits rose slightly, that was only half a mile away.

'Alright, you lot,' I said, sounding confident, 'if we can get him in my van we'll take him home.'

It was a big 'if', I thought, as I reversed the dog van towards Archie. A low-loader would have been more useful than a Mini-van, especially a Mini-van split down the middle by a partition. However, we could but try.

I opened the two rear doors of the van, and then hastily shut and bolted the offside door as Triton tried to launch himself on the assembled company.

'Geddown you bugger,' I shouted, 'GET DOWN.'

Triton subsided slowly onto his rear haunches, but kept himself in such a position so that he could keep a careful eye out of his back window.

Then we gathered round Archie, who had begun to snore loudly. Lucky devil, I thought, all this trouble he's causing me and he won't know anything about in the morning.

As it turned out I was to be proved wrong. I poked the recumbent Archie with my foot, and saw ripples of fat roll back and forth across his enormous stomach. It couldn't be put off any longer.

'O.K. fellahs,' I said, 'let's get him in.'

We all took a piece of Archie and lifted and with much grunting and bad language, staggered toward the nearby van. Archie's head and shoulders slid into the Mini-van easily enough and then he stuck. The combination of his great fat belly at the front, and his huge backside, were not designed to fit into the nearside of Mini-vans.

We were also at a mechanical disadvantage, being unable to control the top half of Archie, which was now firmly wedged in the van. Then Triton intervened. He had watched with disgust the upper part of Archie slide past him, but a few words from me had kept him in the down position. When however, Archie's rear end bulged into HIS side of HIS van, it was all too much.

I should explain at this point the internal geography of the early dog vans to those used nowadays, the latter having fitted chromium-plated cages with separate interior doors and all facilities provided to keep a police dog in a secure and happy environment. The Mini-vans we had then had a wire grill fitted behind the seats, looking suspiciously like part of a baker's bread tray.

Precariously bracketed to this construction was a double hardboard partition somewhat shakily fitted down the middle of the van designed, more in hope than anything else, to keep warring police dogs apart - not always successfully. The main design fault, we had found, was that the partition had a straight edge at the rear, due probably to the inability of the police carpenter to do 'round bits'. As the back doors on a Mini-van curve gracefully from top to bottom inside, this left a gap between the end of the partition and the doors.

It was through this gap that Archie bulged. With one bite and a deceptively casual snatch of his head, Triton severed Archie's belt and waistband of his trousers.

With his second bite he removed a large piece of Archie's trousers, exposing a large piece of Archie's flesh.

Despite a despairing 'NO, LEAVE HIM,' from me, with his third bite Triton sunk his teeth deep into Archie's backside. I have seen hardened criminals break down and cry when Triton bit them. Archie didn't move, didn't blink, didn't respond. His trousers, already under considerable strain, gave up the ghost and collapsed round his ankles, rendering Archie an even more unpalatable sight.

Accepting that he wouldn't fit in the van, we heaved and strained once more and deposited Archie back in the gutter. With impeccable timing, Archie was sick. We rolled him into the semi-prone position and wearily straightened up. I toyed with the idea of calling out the public works and asking them to erect barriers round him till the morning, but decided I must stop fantasizing and do something.

Salvation arrived in an unlikely form. With a roaring engine a corporation bus shot down the main road, the roaring rising to a scream as the driver executed one of those snappy gear changes of which only bus drivers are capable. Only briefly checking his speed at the junction, the driver nursed his vehicle round the traffic island at the maximum possible rate of knots, the bus leaning dangerously as he did so.

With a squeal of brakes and the crunch of tyres the bus halted at the nearby stop and the engine died to a steady throb as the driver jumped out and stood impatiently by the clock with his key ready. I knew, without being told, that the only buses that travelled that fast in Birmingham were those on their way back to the depot. I had an idea.

'Er, driver,' I called.

A cheerful West Indian face turned to me.

'Yes man - well now, how you doing?'

Even better, he recognized me. I remembered then, I had thrown two drunks off his bus a couple of months before.

'Er, I need a favour,' I said, 'it's worth a drink.'

The driver looked with interest at Archie. 'Is that the favour?' he said, with the whites of his eyes showing all round the pupils.

I nodded, 'He lives by the bus garage. We'll get him on and get him off. How about it?'

'OK man,' the driver laughed, 'why not?'

'Right you lot,' I said to Archie's mates, 'half a dollar each now, for the driver, you can get it back off Archie tomorrow.'

They nodded and dipped in their pockets. I handed the driver about thirty bob in assorted coins and we addressed ourselves to the problem of Archie with renewed vigour. Once again we all took hold of various parts of him, and lifting him out of the gutter, lurched down the length of the bus and successfully and without great difficulty loaded him onto the low front platform.

The driver punched his key in the clock, and after looking cautiously round for any sight of his Inspector, climbed over Archie and into his seat. Six of Archie's mates jumped on the bus, and after cautiously looking round for MY inspector, I got into the dog van and followed the bus up the road. I noted with interest that Archie's feet were hanging off the platform and hoped the driver didn't cut his corners too closely.

Archie's house was only eighty yards from the bus depot, and it took only a brief pause by the driver and we had Archie off in the twinkling of an eye. The finishing post was in sight. One of the lads jumped over the back gate, apparently from long practice, and shortly after re-appeared opening Archie's front door. He should have double doors fitted, we decided, as we all tried to fit through the gap, now all in a panic to get rid of our burden before our arms dropped off.

Finally and gratefully we dropped, none too gently I may say, the still unconscious Archie in his hallway. Any thoughts about getting him up the stairs to bed were instantly discarded and never voiced. We rolled him over again into the semi-prone position. I didn't want him choking to death overnight, I could just imagine the horrendous complications if that happened.

'You did what, Officer? On a bus? I see. Hmmm.'

'It's alright mate,' said one of Archie's mates, correctly reading my doubtful looks. 'We'll stay with him till he comes round, he always gets pissed of a week-end but not usually this bad.'

'Well, he's in a right bloody state tonight,' I replied. 'What ever possessed him to get like this?'

'It's being so fat's the problem, you see, he can't pick up no birds; drinking is the only pleasure he gets.'

'It was all quiet outside the New Inns, Mac,' I radioed in, 'I'm clearing'.

I returned to the van and wearily flopped into the driver's seat. I turned my head and looked back at Triton who was happily chewing at a piece of torn denim. He paused in his labours and raised his eyes to mine. From the look of deep satisfaction on his face, it was obviously his considered opinion that a shredded pair of jeans gave infinitely more enjoyment than 20 pints of lager could ever do. On balance I had to agree, he was probably right.

# CHAPTER FOUR

## *EARLY DAYS*

Triton hadn't always been the size of a brick outhouse, of course. When I first saw him he was a rather leggy and thin Alsatian pup about ten months old.

'That's your dog, kid. Take him for a walk and get to know each other.' Hutch, the training sergeant, then promptly disappeared for one of his frequent tea breaks, leaving Triton and I regarding each other doubtfully.

The day before, Triton had been ruling the roost in a family home in Cirencester. And the biggest dog I had ever owned was a small collie bitch. Now, because of some drastic indiscretion concerning the local postman, Triton found himself in the 'jail' of our kennel block, surrounded by large barking dogs and even larger, shouting men. I had no excuse, I was a volunteer.

I plucked up courage and opened the kennel door. Triton growled at me for the first and last time. I quickly grabbed his choke chain and clipped his lead on as if it were something I was completely used to, and took him outside. He pulled away from me and I jerked him in to heel with a loud shout. He pulled away again. I pulled him in again.

We progressed up the field in a similar fashion to the 'Hokey Cokey', in-out, until suddenly Triton no longer pulled away and walked nicely to heel. His deep, brown eyes met mine as if to say, 'OK, round one to you fellah,' and unknown to both of us, it was the start of a magical partnership that was to last for the next thirteen years.

Under Hutch's guidance, I soon learnt the easy ways of teaching a dog basic obedience.

Finding out, for example, that dogs don't understand English, but that if you put a dog in a certain position and repeat the appropriate command often enough, the dog will eventually automatically do the correct thing when you say so...most of the time.

But although most obedience is a bit of a bore, it is essential for the handler to be completely in charge of the dog. If it's the other way round, you've got big problems. I always say that dogs are like women, you've got to stay on top of them all the time (sorry, darling, joke).

Once a dog has learned to be reasonably obedient you can teach him to bite people. Triton enjoyed this. On his first test bite, instead of the usual tentative chew of a piece of sacking wrapped round the instructor's arm, Triton crashed on and took a full-bloodied bite round Hutch's forearm and dug in.

With no proper arm-guard on for the younger dogs, Hutch must have been in a fair bit of physical discomfort, if not pain, but he grinned, 'You're going to have no trouble with that little bastard, he's a natural.' And he was right, all through his next ten years of police work Triton never failed to stop a fleeing criminal. Not that every person we arrested had to be bitten, of course, very often the mere threat of Triton's teeth was enough to make even a determined man hastily re-appraise a snap decision to make a break for it.

But all that was in the future. There was still a multitude of things for us both to learn before we were let loose on the long-suffering general public of Birmingham. Like, for example, how to get a young, fit dog to come back to you, when you've let him off the lead.

A young, fit dog moreover, who can run three times as fast as you and who is having a whale of a time running round and round a big holly bush expertly keeping his collar just beyond the reach of my fingertips. I was getting hotter and hotter and madder and madder. I could see Triton was laughing at me as he jerked away for the umpteenth time.

Panicky thoughts went through my mind. 'Suppose I never get him back? I've only had him three days. What if he runs away?' But then I came to my senses and started to think clearly.

I remembered what Hutch had said to another dog handler, 'Don't chase him lad - make him chase you.'

Of course! Instead of running round in circles, I took off up the field away from Triton and surprise, surprise, it worked. Triton came charging up after me and when he jumped up to play with my wrist it was a simple matter to grab him and my heartbeat could return to normal.

It was little incidents like this which made me aware of the depth of knowledge that Hutch possessed, seemingly simple things once you know them, but all put together to make the training of a dog an easier and more pleasurable experience.

Like teaching a dog to bark. Teach a dog to bark? Don't be daft, every dog can bark, but the trick is making the dog bark when you, the owner, want him to and not just when he feels like it. I guarantee that anytime any dog barks anywhere, someone, somewhere, will tell it to SHUT UP. This will lead eventually to the dog being frightened to bark when he is supposed to and he will let the burglars in.

With our young police dogs, every time they bark they are praised, and the work of command SPEAK is repeated over and over again while they are actually barking. This leads the dog to associate in his mind the command 'speak' with the fact that he is barking and after a few weeks, sometimes months, instead of the dog barking and the handler saying 'speak', the whole thing reverses itself and the handler can say 'speak' and the dog will bark. It's all to do with an association of ideas. The penny dropped with Triton quite quickly, he liked barking very much. The trick was to be able to shut him up. I was still trying when he retired ten years later.

# CHAPTER FIVE

## *A NOSE FOR IT*

Contrary to general belief, the most important and useful part of a police dog isn't his teeth, it's his nose. With his nose a trained dog can do a number of things far beyond the capabilities of mere mortals, into which category fit most policemen.

As Hutch led Triton and I through the basics of tracking and searching he kept hammering into me the golden rule of nose-work that 'The dog MUST enjoy it or he won't do it.' There can be none of the shouting and lead-jerking of the obedience field or criminal work arena, just soft encouragement and exuberance to guide the dog along the track until he realizes what it is you want him to do.

There is nothing complicated about laying a track. For a novice dog it simply means the trainer walking 80 yards or so in a straight line through longish grass carrying a play-article which the dog knows is in his possession. The play-thing is then put down at the end of the track, and on the return of the trainer the dog is encouraged to go and find it.

The handler controls the dog by means of a harness reserved for tracking, to which is attached a long line. Most keen dogs rush off in a blaze of curiosity and it is up to the handler to steady things down a bit and steer the dog onto the line of scent left by the track-layer.

The trick is to convince the dog that you can track better than he can. Once he thinks this is so, being your obedient servant, he will perform miracles for you and be able to follow exactly where someone has walked, some considerable time later. Not always , of course.

There are many factors which may foul or destroy a line of scent because, when they are tracking, dogs do not follow the scent of the man. What they follow is the scent of the ground that the man disturbs as he walks.

If a person walks across a field of grass, every time he puts a foot down as he walks, he bends, breaks or bruises a couple of dozen blades of grass. As this grass is bent, bruised or broken it gives off the scent of disturbed grass, and after a few minutes each foot-print shaped piece of scent combines together to form a continuous line of scent.

Just as we could see a line of foot-prints in the snow with our eyes, so a dog can visualize a line of foot-prints in the grass with his nose.

As the dog progresses beyond the very basic stage of a straight line, a right-angled turn is taken at the end of the first leg, and it is up to the handler to slow his dog down near the corner and steer him in the new direction. It is amazingly hilarious to watch the mess a novice handler and young dog can get into just by the apparently simple manoeuvre of turning a corner. The thirty feet or so of tracking line can get quickly tangled round the legs of dogs and humans who don't really know what they are doing.

More than once I ended up flat on my backside in wet grass due to a careless loop left round my ankles. And Triton was always getting the damn thing round his neck or standing there pitifully with one hind leg stuck out, track forgotten, as he thrashed about trying to free himself from a stray loop of line.

Fortunately dogs and humans both have brains, and as I learnt to hold the line high as he was circling, so Triton learned to duck under it if it did go slack, and proper management of the line became second nature to both of us. I tried to keep a steady and light pressure behind him with no jerking, using my right forearm as a type of spring while Triton did his bit at the front with his nose.

After a week or two we began to get the hang of things and once I stopped getting hot and flustered and began to have confidence in my dog, that confidence seemed to go down the line to Triton. He in turn began to put his nose down firmly to the ground and, with his tail wagging gently, set off in the correct direction.

It was a good indication, his tail. When he picked up the line of scent it would wave about gently and happily. If he lost the track it would droop unhappily to start with, then stick out rigidly as he hunted about in determined fashion to find it again.

When he did find it, as he nosed onto it, his tail would stick straight upright in triumph for a couple of seconds and then resume its slow side-to-side motion.

I'd learnt something else, I was beginning to 'read' my dog.

While tracking was carried out under the control of a harness and line, searching for a hidden person is a much more flamboyant affair. To start with the dog is allowed to see the man disappear into the bushes or whatever, and after a few seconds pause to allow curiosity to build, he is permitted to run up on the lead with the handler and investigate.

Once he finds the man in hiding, he in turn encourages the dog to bark at him while the handler controls his dog to stop him biting out of excitement. Once the control is established, which usually takes a week or two, the exercise is developed to a search off the lead.

Triton loved this. Once I had shouted the standard sort of challenge, 'This is the police, come out or I'll send my dog', his back end would rise trembling with excitement from the sitting position. He would assume a sort of squat, like a sprinter in the blocks, as if to try and persuade me he really was still sitting, even though his backside was at least six inches off the ground. At my next command, 'Go on son, find him' he would take off with all the acceleration of a startled hare and charge wildly about the landscape, hunting his quarry.

The scent coming from a man hiding out of doors drifts with the wind in exactly the same manner as smoke drifts from a garden fire. Just as we could find a bonfire by following the smoke to where it is thickest, so a dog can find a hidden person by following the scent to where it is strongest.

It was fascinating to watch my dog, one moment in full flight up a field, suddenly jack-knife to his right into the wind and then carefully, with his nose in the air, follow the invisible drift of scent to where the man was concealed.

Even now, after more than twenty years as a dog handler, I can still remember the thrill and pride I felt when Triton found his first real-life prisoner.

It wasn't much of a call really, it wasn't even much of a difficult search, but I'll never forget it.

An old lady in a ground floor flat in Moseley had heard a slight noise outside her bedroom window while she was getting ready for bed. When she had peered through her curtains she found herself face to face with a young man who had been doing a bit of peeping through the crack. It would have been difficult to sort out who was the more frightened. The old lady screamed, the young man gasped and fell backwards through the rose bushes, before scrambling away.

It would have been so easy to presume he had kept going and was probably now safely tucked up in his bed, but I have always been prepared to put a bit of extra trouble into my job, even if there was only a slim chance of a prisoner. With Triton on the lead I searched the old lady's back garden until Triton pulled me through a gap in the hedge at the bottom.

With his nose down he tracked across the next garden and jumped over the low fence into the next. While I was scrambling over the fence he suddenly jerked the lead out of my hand and angled quickly across to a hawthorn hedge on the far side of this, the third garden.

In the gloom I could see him suspiciously sniffing at the hedge until the hedge made a rustling noise. Triton jumped back a pace, startled, and involuntarily started barking.

I was with him by now, and I in turn was startled when a head stuck up out of the hedge and said 'I give in'. It was bloody magic, absolutely wonderful, I was on cloud nine. I gave Triton a massive hug and a great deal of fuss as our Peeping Tom tried to extricate himself from the hawthorn. I overcame my euphoria enough to help him out and took him back to the other lads, trying very hard to keep the grin off my face, but I couldn't.

It had been a very special experience, Triton's first prisoner. I was not to know it then, but it was the first of many.

# CHAPTER SIX

## *GONE FOR A BURTON*

Probationary Constables materialize as two types. Those that can and those that can't. Those that do and those that don't. For some months we had been experimenting with an unofficial attachment of the odd pro-con to the Dog Section. It was a very informal affair involving any spare young officer going out on patrol with the night dog handler so they could see how we worked. We, as dog men, could in return provide his Inspector with a different angle for his assessment reports. It also gave us someone fresh to stuff into cupboards or climb trees for the dogs to search and find. It gave an extra edge to their scenting exercises when their quarry was displaying genuine fear (we always like to see new blood on the Dog Section).

John, the lad who I had with me on this particular week of nights was the son of our recently retired Detective Inspector and, therefore, perhaps keener to please than most. The Monday night had been deader than dead, and I had taken the opportunity to do a bit of night training with Triton, with John willingly concealing himself in railway trucks on Bordesley sidings, and later tramping off down the canal towpath in the pitch black, all for Triton's benefit. Triton wasn't daft of course. Like all our dogs he knew when it was a training exercise and treated John with proper decorum when he found him, merely barking six inches from his nose, rather than actually dragging him out of his hiding place by whatever bit he could get hold of.

By midnight on Tuesday I was beginning to get a bit desperate for a call. I had been regaling John with various stories about Triton's prisoners and how exciting it was being a dog handler, and there we were, well into our second night, without even a sniff so to speak.

For something to do, I went and parked up in the entrance to the railway yard which served as an unofficial car park for the local Irish Strip Club. I concealed my anonymous little Mini-van in between two of several battered tipper lorries and settled down to keep observations on the parked cars. There had been a spate of thefts from this car park a few weeks ago, but it had tailed off. Still, worth a try.

The gods smiled on me. John and I had barely finished our first cigarette when a small dark figure started mooching among the cars. We could just see from where we were that he was trying the door handles and quarter lights. Triton sensed the electric atmosphere in the van and started to whimper. 'Quiet', I hissed. John reached for the door catch. 'Wait', I said hoarsely, 'wait until he's done a bit more.'

This was a new experience for me, trying to restrain two impatient young things. Finally, at about his tenth car, the small dark shape forced an insecure quarter light, opened the door and disappeared inside. 'Right', I said, let's get him'.

John was out of the van and gone like greased lightening. I didn't expect to have to use Triton in these circumstances, but I got him out anyway and ran over. It was John's first prisoner ever, for crime, and he had pounced like a hungry lion.

The little prospective car thief was in a very efficient arm lock and was squeaking like a stuck pig. 'Don't break his arm, John' I said, 'not unless he struggles, anyway. Have you cautioned him and told him why he's been arrested?' John looked at me blankly. I repeated what I had said and I could see the light dawn on John's face.

He more or less said the right things while I checked inside the car. Ignition barrel unscrewed and wires hanging down under the dashboard was enough, and I radioed for a panda to take our prisoner into Bradford Street Police Station.

When it arrived, John escorted his prisoner in triumph and I strolled over to the Strip Club to find the owner of the car.

I knew Mick, the doorman, quite well and while he disappeared inside on my errand I viewed the show through the glass panel in the double doors.

Very tasteful tattoos, I thought, but then the car's owner anxiously scuttled out and I had to return to the car park. A few minutes spent rewiring and taking details and I followed on into the nick.

It took us a couple of hours to deal with our prospective car thief and after a quick cup of tea and a sandwich we didn't get out again until nearly 3.00 am. John was still bubbling with enthusiasm after his first arrest and was in an irrepressible mood. We had a cruise up to the top end of the Division and were rewarded with an alarm call at a multiple tailors in Acocks Green village. It took me about four minutes of hard driving to reach the shop and I used the time to remind John of the golden rule when the dog is working - 'Don't get in the way.'

The glass in the shop doorway was broken and I kicked the remaining bits off the bottom rail and quickly cleared the worst fragments from the floor. The first two officers at the premises had done their job properly and were guarding the escape routes, so I called an impatient Triton from where he was sitting on the forecourt and he leapt through the hole into the shop. I ducked through after him and watched him start hunting through the racks of suits and shirts on the extensive shop floor.

I shone my torch round the walls, looking for the light switches. But, as in most large stores, they appeared to be hidden away somewhere, so I carried on by torchlight and the dim glow of the street lights feeding in through the shop windows. I could hear Triton as he went off the carpeted aisles onto the parquet floor and back again.

His searching had steadied from his initial charge round the place and we methodically worked our way from the front to the rear. Triton reached the glass-sided floor manager's office a few feet in front of me and, as he got to the far corner, I saw him stiffen and he let out a low growl as he launched himself sideways round the back of the office.

As I swung my torch round, I heard a tremendous smashing of glass and could see the blurred outline of a man struggling to get through the window into the far side of the office. All the glass was frosted so I couldn't see very clearly, but it sounded as if Triton was having a fair battle with his prisoner.

I ran round the corner of the square office partition shouting 'Hold him son' and then stopped and burst out laughing 'You dozy pillock,' I said to Triton, 'just look what you've done. Look at the mess'. Triton let go of his 'prisoner' and looked at me puzzled at the change in my voice. Why wasn't I my usual delighted self when he'd caught a prisoner?

I'll tell you why I'm not my usual delighted self, I said, reading his mind, 'it's because you've just savaged a bloody tailor's dummy that's why'. I've got to admit that with the top hat, Crombie overcoat and collar and tie under a smart dark suit, the dummy had looked like a man standing in the gloom. It didn't look so smart now though. The hat brim was full of glass, the Crombie was ripped and there was a hole in the right knee of the suit where Triton had grabbed it and pulled the dummy over with such spectacular results.

There was then a further complication. John's voice came from the front door, 'Keyholder's arrived, Steve. Do you want him in or have you got something, I heard all the noise'. I expect half the neighbourhood heard it, I thought. I decided honesty was the best policy. 'Yes, bring him in', I shouted.

As I explained what had happened, the keyholder looked at the window, then at the dummy and finally at me and Triton. He looked serious and said, 'Well it's a proper mess'. I looked suitably contrite and nodded my head in agreement.

To my relief the keyholder's face broke into a broad grin. 'Sorry', he said, 'just winding you up. The firm can afford it and I'll get free drinks out of this for weeks. It'll make a wonderful story down at the golf club'.

I looked at John's face and realised it was going to make a wonderful story in the police canteen as well. But you can't win 'em all.

# CHAPTER SEVEN

## *TRITON AND THE ITALIAN JOB*

'You attacka my wife, I keel you!'  The gentleman of Italian appearance did not look pleased.  When I first saw him he was waving a large carving knife above his head and shouting at the four young men he was chasing.  One of these men was carrying a woman's shopping bag, and although I never exactly qualified for the graduate entry scheme, I instantly and correctly guessed what had happened.

Police Dog Triton in his cage behind me wasn't a graduate entry either, and he was on to what was happening even quicker than I was, and began barking deafeningly in my right ear, hoping no doubt that I would let him out there and then.  He obviously felt confident enough to deal with the matter on his own.

The four youths, closely pursued by our Italian friend, had by now disappeared up the next side street on my left having crossed in front of me.  Somehow I managed to transmit, 'Robbery in progress, Clifton Road,' change down into second gear AND spin the dog van round the left hand corner without tying myself in a knot.  The total boredom of a quiet Sunday evening in Balsall Heath was transformed within a matter of seconds.

In Clifton Road I was confronted with the sight of our now rapidly tiring Italian seeing his wife's attackers getting away from him.  I was a bit limited in my options and decided to drive straight past the four muggers to give me room for manoeuvre and then jump out with Triton and see what transpired.

Birmingham City Police had dark blue unmarked dog vans in those days and this gave me a few seconds' grace as I shot past our four heroes, now confidently increasing the distance between themselves and their angry pursuer.  It came as a severe shock to their systems when they found their escape blocked as I stood the dog van on its nose about 50 yards in front of them.

I leapt out after fortunately remembering to set the hand brake. I say fortunately because it has been known for the over enthusiastic officer to forget such mundane details in the heat of the moment and be forced to suffer the embarrassment of watching his driverless police vehicle wreak havoc amongst the local population's prized possessions.

As I ran to the back doors of the dog van to release Triton and thereby even the numbers up a bit, I saw that three of them had hesitated, while the fourth, wearing a yellow T-shirt, and obviously a thinker, had kept going at full speed and was now in fact already past me.

The three who had hesitated now became aware of the increasing volume of Italian oaths approaching from their rear and, coming to a quick unspoken collective decision, decided it would probably be easier to get past me and started in my direction.

Then I got Triton out of the van and their decision suddenly didn't look so good after all. It was a brave man who would take Triton on from the front end and their courage and choices seemed to be running out.

One of them leapt sideways and I swear that he cleared a five-foot gate into an entry without touching it, while the second ran across the road and round the back of some houses, leaving me facing the biggest of the three, still holding the shopping bag. Triton looked round and saw yellow T-shirt still going strong in the middle of the road and I could see that he had made his decision, so I let him go and have his fun while I turned my attention to the remaining young man.

Seeing Triton chase off after his unfortunate partner in crime gave number four renewed confidence, and dropping the bag he came at me, head down, with every intention of running right through me and away.

Now while not even my best friends would say that I was the greatest rugby player that ever lived, and like most front row forwards, I am an absolute sucker for a nifty side-step, again like most front row forwards, nobody ever ran through me and got away with it.

I tackled number four nicely round the knees and he hit the pavement like a ton of bricks, knocking all the wind and fight out of him. I clambered on top of his back and grabbed an arm. 'You're nicked mate,' I said, and looked up to see what Triton was doing.

I was just in time to see my dog take off and bite yellow T-shirt on the right arm, while still in mid-air. The results of a heavy dog like Triton hitting a man at full speed should really carry a Government health warning. Suddenly having ninety odd pounds of dog firmly attaching itself to your arm tends to upset the balance and it was interesting to see yellow T-shirt do a complete cartwheel and end up flat on his back with Triton still hanging on.

While in the middle of his enforced gymnastics, yellow T-shirt gave out the loudest yell I have ever heard, difficult to describe in print, but rather like the red-skins used to shout as they bit the dust in my old cowboy comics.

AAA...III...EEE... was something like it. Triton let go of his arm and, putting both paws on his chest, looked enquiringly into his face to see if anything was wrong. The yelling stopped.

Then I made a mistake, understandable maybe, but nevertheless a mistake. 'Good lad', I shouted, 'Hold him, stay there.' Triton looked back at me and saw, I suppose, that I was on the floor and struggling with a man. Abandoning yellow T-shirt he came running back toward me and, in spite of my pleas to stop, came crashing in and bit the young man I was sitting on.

'No, not this one, that one,' I said despairingly, and pointed to where yellow T-shirt was unsteadily getting to his feet. Triton looked and ran back at yellow T-shirt and, without biting him, hit him behind the knees so that he was up-ended and flat on his back once more. This time he didn't try to get up.

Now a further complication arrived in the form of an irate Italian husband. 'You hold heem still, I cut his throat. He attacka my wife.' He was very excited.

'Yes, yes,' I said hastily, 'that's enough. Nobody's going to kill anybody here. I'll deal with it if you don't mind. Put the knife away, there's a good lad.'

Fortunately other officers arrived before my prisoner was dismembered, and our Italian calmed down enough to tell us what had happened when he saw his wife knocked down and robbed as she turned into her front path. The other two young men we arrested later after what are laughingly called 'routine enquiries', making the score four-nil to the goodies for once.

The Italian was a good witness in court and refused to be shaken in cross-examination. I remember one phrase he used which raised a few smiles in the court, even in the defence camp.

'Oh ze dog', he had said, spreading his arms in an admiring fashion, 'Ze dog, he ees manifico.' And looking at Triton later that evening, gently playing with my youngest son in the garden, and remembering yellow T-shirt's flying cartwheel, I had to agree, he was - manifico.

# CHAPTER EIGHT

## *TRANSPORTS OF DELIGHT*

As our old and faithful Mini-van passed the 95,000 milestone it began to suffer an increasing number of prospectively terminal complaints. It was, of course, to be expected. You cannot mercilessly thrash what is basically a standard small delivery vehicle without something giving.

What did start to give with monotonous regularity was the floor under the driver's seat. We had got used to seeing the road surface flashing past through the hole by the driver's right heel, but judicious positioning of the rubber mat tended to hide that at service time. What none of us was prepared to risk, however, was being deposited onto the road via the ever-widening crack where the rear seat supports were supposed to be resting on the floor. Several years of the six dog handlers on our Division, flopping the last two feet down onto the seat every time they got into the van, had taken a heavy toll on the resilience of the floor panelling.

The head foreman at the garage shook his head slowly when he saw the plank of wood we had wedged across the underside of the seat frame. 'I'm sorry, lads' he said. 'It won't do. She'll have to be done properly this time. There'll be all hell to pay if it has an accident in that state. Phone me in a week. Might be ready then.

A week, we thought, ye gods, a whole week without our van. 'Why so serious?' I hear the 1990s style police officer say. Simply nip down to the transport pool and borrow a spare, or phone the adjacent Division and borrow one of theirs. Why all the portents of doom and despond?

I'll explain to the cossetted and pampered modern officer the depth of the despondency. In the seventies, Birmingham City Police had six Divisions and six dog vans.

When yours went off the road, that was it. No spare, no nothing. Well not quite. What we had to do, and I still feel a shiver go down my back as I write these words, was to borrow the despatch van.

It was, I admit, a set of wheels and better than nothing. During the day it pottered round the seven police stations on the Division, delivering the internal paperwork. Including one trip to Force Headquarters in the morning run, and the odd diversion to the Chief Superintendent's house with the Divisional motor mower, it very rarely exceeded 40 miles per day and NEVER exceeded 40 miles per hour.

It was the jealously guarded toy of the Admin staff and the last thing they wanted was big, wet, hairy, muddy police dogs in the back and Stirling Moss style maniacal, heathen dog handlers in the front.

As our Mini-van aged more and more, we were forced to borrow the despatch van with increasing frequency, much to the annoyance of the Admin Inspector, an individual who regarded himself as second only to God, who in those days resided in the Chief Superintendent's office.

The Inspector's complaints had become more numerous and increasingly bitter. He would pompously say something like, 'The Chief Constable wants to know why there were dog hairs adhering to the Chief Superintendent's monthly report', or, 'There was mud all over the passenger seat this morning, my uniform was in a disgusting mess. I shall report the night dog man to the Chief". We knew, however, there was little danger of this as he only wore his full uniform when he wanted a discount on one of his 'shopping' trips.

Or the more dramatic, 'There is blood all over the head lining'.

Slightly dodgy one this, as we knew that Ken and his dog had had a desperate and so far unpublicized battle with a violent drunken prisoner half-way back to the nick. Then Charlie had one of his bright ideas and explained it away as his dog having cut his ear and flicked blood everywhere, unnoticed in the dark. As with every incident, we mumbled abject apologies and raced out to the yard to clean up the mess.

But this time he said, 'A week! You're not having it for a week and that's that', and at two minutes to four every afternoon he locked the van keys in his safe and went home.

He didn't reckon on his dog men. We resorted to Plan B. When the coast was clear at ten minutes past four we used the excellent set of car keys we had liberated from one of our better car thieves and we were mobile again.

We were found out, of course. One glance at the vehicle logbook was a dead giveaway, but we emerged from the resultant soft stuff with a definite authorisation from on high to use the vehicle when necessary. Which brought us to the biggest predicament of all. The one thing we could do nothing about, given all our resourcefulness - the van was a Morris 1000.

Now whatever attributes this particular model had as a means of transporting a modest amount of goods about the place in a steady reliable fashion, as a police dog van (albeit temporary) it was an absolute pig.

It took an age to work up any head of steam. At relatively modest speeds it rolled frighteningly round corners, not helped by having approximately one hundredweight of police dog sliding uncontrollably from side to side. And there was no cage fitted in the back, as the new young watch Inspector at Bradford Street police station found out one night.

I usually took Triton up to the canteen with me for my 2.00 am coffee break. There he would either snooze beside me next to the easy chair or lay his chin on the table eyeing the lads' food as they ate it.

He became quite partial to mouthfuls of anything from Madras curry to cheese sandwiches, but nobody minded and it didn't seem to do him any harm. On this night, however, it had been sheeting down with rain and he was absolutely soaked, so rather than risk upsetting the much-feared Maggie, the station cleaner, I left him lying in the back of the van, gently steaming.

The Inspector was due off duty at 2.00 am for a ten o'clock court appearance and dashed out into the back yard into the rain at about twenty past.

With a flash of annoyance he saw that the despatch van was blocking his car in, but noticed the glint of the ignition keys swinging in the centre of the dashboard. He opened the door and leapt in, reaching for the keys.

With his own activities and the drumming of the rain on the roof masking other sounds, he first realized he wasn't alone when he felt hot breath on his neck and heard a soft growl terrifyingly close to his left ear. For a few seconds the Inspector froze and then, very, very slowly, inched his head round to his left. Triton's eyes were normally a deep soft brown, but in the glow of the yard lights they seemed to have a reddish tinge. To the Inspector they looked to be blazing at him. 'What are you doing in my van?' they said. He moved his hand slowly towards the door handle. Triton growled softly again. He moved his hand away and sat there, unmoving.

Fifteen minutes later a double-manned Panda swung into the yard and parked next to my van. As the observer jumped out with his head down against the rain he caught a glimpse of the Inspector's white face looking at him beseechingly through the driver's window.

He paused, 'Are you all right, gaffer?' he shouted through the glass.

Triton's bark at the newcomer explained all. The Inspector's face went whiter. Silently he mouthed, 'Get the effing dog man down here. Now!'

Once safely out of sight of the van, the Panda crew collapsed in each others' arms, absolutely helpless. Still shaking with laughter, tears streaming down their faces, they staggered up the stairs and burst into the canteen.

'Steve', gasped Mike, the driver, 'the gaffer's in your van, with...with your dog'. He was unable to speak any further. Indeed considering the state of him, it was remarkable he managed to convey as much as he did.

While the rest of the shift rushed to the canteen windows, I raced anxiously down the stairs, praying the gaffer was still in one piece. I opened the van door and saw two faces staring at me, both pleased to see me.

'Get down, son,' I said to Triton, and 'You can get out now, gaffer' to the Inspector. He slowly climbed out of the van and stood facing me.

'Are you OK, sir?' I said, trying to ignore the line of grinning faces I could see behind him up at the canteen window.

He must have seen my eyes flicker upwards and he turned and glared at our audience. By the time he turned back to me I was having the greatest difficulty in keeping the grin off my face.

'I suppose the whole nick knows by now', he said. I nodded, I didn't dare speak for fear of laughing out loud. The stiffness went from him and he suddenly relaxed and started to smile faintly.

'They never mentioned how to deal with THAT at Staff College,' he said. 'Come on, I need a cup of tea. And you're paying', he added over his shoulder.

On a fun-to-cost ratio, it was well worth it.

# CHAPTER NINE

## *BY DAWN'S EARLY LIGHT*

I hate earlies. Whether you call it first watch, morning shift or early turn, I still hate them. It's simply not natural to get out of a warm bed before five o'clock in the morning only to blunder about in the bathroom, praying that you don't cut yourself shaving and bleed all over your last clean shirt. Then you shuffle about in the kitchen scooping cold milk and cereal into your mouth while waiting for the kettle to boil. Finally you pour half of the scalding hot mug of tea down your cold throat, throw the remainder down the sink and go out to face the day.

Triton used to watch me go through this routine from his comfy corner of the kitchen. As he matured and became wiser in the ways of humans, he has learned that they - especially this one - were not at their best at 5.15am. He had found out I was not at all keen on the big welcome - paws on chest, facewash with his tongue - before dawn had broken. I know it's unfair but - yes, I admit it - it made me irritable.

Now at the wise old age of six, his early morning acknowledgement of my presence was much more decorous. The nearest ear would cock towards me. The eyes would swivel round, but his head would not move and the end six inches of his tail would gently wave up and down while the rest of it lay still on the floor.

'Hello son' I would say. A moment's pause would follow while Triton absorbed the tone of my voice. Then, having judged it safe to do so, he would slowly rise and stretch first his front legs, then his back legs, lift his chin, wag his tail and allow me to fondle the top of his head.

This routine complete, it was on with the coat and out to the car.

The journey was gauged exactly to arrive at the nick at 5.42am precisely - just in time for the unit's parade and briefing. In the 1970's, this was a much more relaxed affair than it had been when I joined the service in 1965.

The youngest officer on the shift made the tea, of course, and everyone sat round the table in leisurely fashion, only half absorbing their area postings, refreshment break times, important car numbers, active disqualified drivers and so on.

Jokes were scarce at this time in the morning; even the shift maniac was quiet. I booked on with force control room; the usual pleasantries were exchanged, 'I'm going over the park for 20 minutes and then I must get on with the rest of that paperwork for the three prisoners we had for burglary last week.' 'OK. We'll try and leave you in peace.'

With Triton walked - only one squirrel to chase that morning - back to the dog section office. I began to write furiously. The one advantage of the first part of the morning shift was the quiet; an ideal time to catch up on reports you never had time for on nights, meant to do on second watch and now really had to get on with. Loads of time, it was only a quarter to seven. The phone rang - my heart sank. Reluctantly I picked up the receiver.

'Steve, it's Barry. We're going to lift Dave the Rave from his drum - 7.15 RV at the Gospel. Can you cover the back in case he does a runner?'

'See you there,' I replied.

A translation would read; 'PC Lewis? This is DC Collins. We are hoping to arrest a Mr David Jackson at his home address. We are rendezvousing at a quarter past seven on the car park of the Gospel Oak Licensed House and we would like you and your dog in the back garden in case Mr Jackson tries to escape.'

But, of course, police officers never talk to each other like that. I gathered the papers spread across the desk and threw them back into the folder with a sigh. What the hell! Who needs reports anyway? Dave the Rave is a much better prospect. He's met Triton before and may still have the scars to prove it. Let's go.

Half an hour later, four CID men in two cars, with me following in the dog van, crept to a halt short of the corner of the cul-de-sac. Triton was positively tingling with excitement. I went first, with Triton on the lead. I tip-toed quickly half way down the cul-de-sac and dashed into the rear alley that gave access to the garages - four houses along and quietly through the broken back gate into the rubbish tip of a garden. Triton and I picked our way carefully towards the house. It was mid-October and still not full light, so I tried to melt into the overgrown privet hedge. A minute passed in silence before a thunderous hammering on the front door.

The noise ceased. Triton strained at his lead, looped round his choke chain ready for instant release. Not a movement in the house, Dave and his family were old hands at this game. More hammering on the front door, and rather un-necessarily,

'Open up, it's the police.'

Right above me, a bedroom window stealthily opened and a leg appeared, followed by a head and arm reaching for the drainpipe. Triton was trembling with anticipation when the man's hand slipped, dislodging some mortar from behind the pipe.

It seemed to crash like thunder in the yard, and I couldn't blame Triton far what he did, I really couldn't. All his pent-up excitement exploded in the loudest bark you ever heard. Mr David Jackson, precariously balanced as he was, nearly fell off the window ledge there and then out of sheer fright. He recovered just in time and sat there swaying. I'm sure I could see his heart beating.

'Excuse me Dave,' I said, 'I think there are some gentlemen at the front door who would like a quick word with you, if you don't mind. There's a good lad.'

I saw him eye up the distance to the outhouse roof.

'Don't even think about it, Dave.' I said, 'Remember last time.'

He grunted: 'Yeah, I remember last time. OK. OK. I'm going.'

Once I knew that the CID had Dave safely in custody, I walked round to the front and waited for the lads to bring him out. As they walked him down the path I saw Triton sniff the air as he caught Dave the Rave's scent.

Triton licked his lips and his mouth half opened in a smile (of course dogs can smile). I'm pretty sure Triton remembered last time as well.

Back in the dog van I looked at my watch; quarter to nine. What with searching the house and one thing and another we'd been there well over an hour. Never mind, still plenty of time to do my paperwork, but first I thought 'Breakfast!'

Yes, Bacon and Egg with all the trimmings and then I could do all those reports in the peace of mid-morning. There would be loads of time, loads……..

The radio bursts into life. 'Foxtrot Tango Six, are you clear yet?'

I hate earlies!

# CHAPTER TEN

## *COMPREHENSIVELY COVERED*

Sunday nights can be funny. Sometimes it seems as if the whole world has gone to bed at 11.30 to prepare for the week's labours. Other Sundays are different. Instead of the opportunity to gently wind down after a week of nights, the by now shattered night-shift officers find themselves dashing from job to job right through to the crack of dawn.

Already by 1.30 am, Police Dog Triton and I had attended five calls with nothing much to show for our efforts. The last one had been an automatic alarm at a large electrical wholesalers on the adjoining division. The key-holder had moaned and groaned about being dragged out of bed. The heating had been going full blast inside the warehouse, making me hot and sweaty, and even Triton was visibly slowing down half-way through the search as the heat got to him. I had filled a hand basin with water for him in the ladies' toilets. From long practice he had jumped up and hooked his front paws over the edge of the basin and almost drank it dry.

At the end of our efforts there was nothing - no break-in, no burglars, just another fault in the system. The key-holder departed, still grumbling, and I let Triton cock his leg in the yard before he jumped back in the dog van.

I dropped into the driver's seat of our Mini-van and started the engine in an effort to get the pathetic little heater working. I was beginning to feel chilly after the warmth of the premises.'

'It's about time we had our coffee break, son,' I said to Triton. 'We'll have a slow drive in, I'm busting for a cuppa.'

Triton looked me in the eyes through the rear view mirror as if he understood every word, although it occurred to me that the gaffer would commit me to the funny farm if he heard me talking to my dog. Still, who else has a lonely dog handler got to talk to?

FOXTROT TANGO SIX, are you clear yet?'

The radio made me jump, I'd turned the volume up while Triton had his run in the yard and forgotten to turn it down again. 'You bastards', I thought. 'Isn't there another sodding dog man on tonight apart from me?'

'Yes, I'm just clearing from the B-Bravo Division,' I said sweetly into the hand-set.

'Ah, good,' said the disembodied voice, 'go to the insurance offices in Moseley. Caller on the nines says she's heard breaking glass at the rear and we've just had the auto alarm come through for the same premises.'

'On my way, four minutes,' I replied.

'Sounds more like it, son,' I said to Triton as I thrashed the dog van through the gears. He in turn started barking with excitement, occasionally breaking off to chew and rip at the central partition. I managed to shut him up before we arrived, but I needn't have worried as the lads on the shift had the place well covered.

'They've done a window at the back, Steve. We think they're still in there and the key-holder will be about 20 minutes.'

I looked at Harry. He was supposed to be canteen man for the night, but had obviously bailed out the nick with the others. Unlike the others, however, he was wearing a long white apron and wielding a huge frying pan.

'Fanny Craddock, I presume,' I said over my shoulder as I grabbed Triton and ran round the back of the offices. The frying pan clattered up the entry after me, startling the young officer standing by the broken window.

I knocked out the rest of the glass with my truncheon and shouted, 'Last chance to give up or the dog's coming in'. Not a sound came from inside, so I climbed over the sill and kicked the glass on the floor away from the window.

'Come on, son,' I said to Triton, and he soared effortlessly through the gap. The effect was spoiled on landing as he spread-eagled on the polished floor and knocked a hat-stand into a glass bookcase as he slid across the room.

'A bull in a china shop has got nothing on us, has it mate,' I said, hastily opening the door into the main corridor.

Triton trotted through and immediately stood stock-still and slowly raised his nose into the air. He swung his head to the left and carefully worked his way along the corridor, his nose still high and about six inches from the right-hand wall. I kept quiet and perfectly still, not wanting to spoil his concentration.

As he reached the door at the end he brought his nose down to the floor and with a snort or two he sniffed deeply at the gap underneath. He pulled his head away and stood with his ears pricked. I saw his tail wag once slowly and I knew what was coming next. There was a low growl followed by a shattering bark as Triton jumped up at the door. As his front legs slid down they pushed the door handle and as he plunged into the room I started to run down the corridor.

A most peculiar sight greeted me in the office. There appeared to be a mythological creature consisting of half man and half dog under one of the desks and it was making a lot of noise. I could see the back legs and tail of Triton sticking out of one side and the head and shoulders of a youth I knew well protruding from the other. He looked a bit like a clown as he was poking through a large sheet of brown paper which the typist had pinned to her desk to keep the draught off her legs. There appeared to be a tug-of-war going on, I could see more and more of Triton until his head appeared with a foot in his mouth.

'Alright son,' I said, ' you've won, leave him.'

Triton let go of the foot which then quickly disappeared back under the desk. 'You can come out now, Dave,' I said, 'consider yourself nicked.'

Our young burglar slowly climbed through the by now tattered piece of brown paper and stood in front of me breathing heavily. 'Where's your brother?' I asked, knowing that they usually did everything together. He looked at me defiantly. 'Dunno, I ain't seen him tonight.'

I stared at him and he lowered his eyes. 'Okay, I said, have it your own way.'

I quickly searched him and took him to the officers at the back of the premises.

'I think there's one more', I said. 'Take him in but keep the place covered.'

With Triton I searched all the rooms in the new building that the insurance brokers had built but with no further success. I finally went down to the front entrance feeling a bit puzzled and frustrated. I knew that Dave nearly always worked with his brother but he certainly wasn't in here. The key-holder came inside when he saw us and I told him my problem.

'How about our old place next door,' he said. 'We still use it for storing files.'

'I tried the connecting door,' I replied, 'but it was locked.'

He looked doubtful. 'Shouldn't be,' he said, 'it's a fire door.'

'The crafty bugger,' I thought, 'he's nipped through and locked it behind him.'

We went outside and round to the other place, which was a converted shop. Once inside I challenged again and off went Triton, apparently tireless. It was amazing how much a good prisoner revived him. I started to follow him and within a couple of minutes I heard him barking upstairs. It sounded different though, not as definite as usual, almost hesitant.

I found him on the landing, running first into a toilet and then across into a storeroom opposite. He seemed confused as if unable to pinpoint the source of the scent. I glanced into the small toilet and then physically searched the storeroom. Nothing. My eyes met Triton's. 'Where is he, son?' I said softly, 'I can't find him'.

Triton looked away and went back into the toilet. This time he put his front paws on the seat and stretched up towards the little window, his nose twitching from side to side. The penny dropped. I climbed onto the toilet seat, stuck my head out of the window and looked up.

'Well, well,' I said, 'Joey, fancy meeting you here. Would you care to step inside?'

'I can't,' came the muffled reply, 'I'm stuck,' and he was.

The Fire Brigade were very good about the interruption to their all-night snooker tournament. They fetched Joey off the roof with hardly any damage to the premises at all.

When our second burglar had been taken away, the key-holder put the kettle on and started to make about 15 cups of tea.

'I'm afraid my dog smashed the glass in the bookcase,' I said, 'and I've cracked the toilet upstairs.'

'And some roof tiles have come down,' said the fire officer, 'and our ladders have broken your guttering at the back.'

'Not to worry,' said the key-holder smiling. 'You'll not be surprised to hear that we're well insured, although with you lot around I feel we may well review our cover.'

You couldn't argue with that.

# CHAPTER ELEVEN

## *A POLICE DOG LOOSE IN A BUTCHER'S SHOP*

Occasionally, just occasionally, the Sod's Law which rules the Police Force relents and the lucky officer may find himself in the right place at the right time.  Thus it was when I received a call from Luscious Lucy in the Control Room (at least her voice sounded like she should be).

'There are two men reported breaking into the butcher's shop in Olton Boulevard East,' came the golden tones over the air.

'I'm pulling up out side the back door now,' I was able to reply, as I was indeed no more than 100 yards away from the shop where the burglary was taking place.

I cut the engine of my trusty Mini-van and coasted quietly into the kerb, with only Police Dog Triton whining softly with excitement to break the silence.  I had long since ceased to wonder how the dogs knew what was going on, what mysterious mechanism stirred them into action without a word being spoken.  Perhaps they could understand the radio?

Nothing would surprise me about dogs anymore.  There were times when Triton seemed a damn sight more intelligent than I was, still, that probably wasn't saying very much.

I left my driver's door open after scrambling out, as the metallic clunk of it shutting would alarm even the doziest of burglars, and grabbed hold of Triton as I opened the rear doors.  Ever keen, he wanted to get on with things without being encumbered by this clumsy human, who tended to get in the way and prevent him from enjoying himself.

'Keep still, you bugger,' I whispered hoarsely as I slipped the lead through his collar so it was ready for instant release and, wasting no more time, ran on tip-toe into the alley at the rear of the parade of shops, crouching below the level of the fence as I reached the butchers.

'Dog man at the rear,' I spoke quietly into my radio, but my voice seemed to echo round the yard.

I peered cautiously round the gatepost, my hand tightening on Triton's collar as he too peered round the gatepost. From my somewhat uncomfortable position I could see that the ground floor window had been broken and opened, and over the hum of the deep-freeze motor I could hear thumping noises inside the shop. We were in business!

I knew that other officers were on the way and decided to wait until we had all the escape routes covered, just to make certain, and sure enough within a minute or so I heard the distinctive scream of the greater spotted Panda at speed as it rounded the corner and squealed to a halt outside the front of the butchers.

Following a double slam of the doors came running footsteps pounding up the entry alongside our shop, materialising in the person of a young policeman. With a fearful roar Triton launched himself at the newcomer, jerking me from my crouching position onto my knees and nearly tearing my fingers off, which were still wrapped round his choke chain. Fortunately the weight of my body stopped Triton about three inches away from ruining the young man's married life, as he in turn went smartly into reverse until he was flattened against the fence.

I spoke first. 'You stupid prat,' I shouted, not being entirely enthralled with having the skin removed from my knees. 'NEVER approach premises like that.' His mouth opened and closed but no sound came. 'Is your mate at the front?' I said, and he nodded. 'Come on then, let's get on with it,' I muttered, and with all need for secrecy now gone I ran down the short backyard with Triton.

'THIS IS THE POLICE,' I shouted, rather unnecessarily, through the window, 'ARE YOU COMING OUT OR WE'LL PUT THE DOG IN?'

There was silence inside. Triton looked at me expectantly and after I quickly checked inside the window he jumped over the sill and was gone. I struggled through after him.

'Stay there,' I said to the hapless young constable, who still hadn't spoken, but the expression on his face indicated that wild horses wouldn't drag him into the shop with the dog loose.

'GOOD LAD,' I shouted. 'FIND HIM. WHERE IS HE?' The familiar phrases used by all dog handlers bounced strangely off the tiled walls.

I could hear the 'Clip, clip, clip' of Triton's claws as he padded round the shop floor and the deep panting noises he gave out when he was searching. Suddenly the noises stopped, which was usually a good sign. They were replaced by a low throaty growl, which was an ever better sign, and as I entered the main part of the shop I was just in time to see Triton's tail disappearing round the back of the counter.

It was all action from then on. There was a loud vibrating bark, quickly followed by an even louder yell, and a scuffling and scrabbling started under the counter. I was there in a second and could see that Triton had hold of an arm which was protruding through a six-inch gap in the sliding doors, and was determinedly trying to pull the rest of his burglar out.

I found out afterwards that the gap had only been an inch, but that Triton had jammed his nose firmly in the small opening and managed to slide the door back far enough to get his head inside. Our unlucky burglar had then found himself literally face-to-face with Triton, and after the first deafening 'WOOF' had thrown up his arm to protect himself, only to have it forcibly seized in a gleaming set of teeth. I ordered Triton to let go, and after a final shake and worry of the arm he had found, he sat and looked at the cupboard rather like the dog on a record label. I slid the door fully open and extracted our terrified burglar.

'You're nicked for burglary, mate,' I said as I walked him to the back of the shop, and I am afraid his reply does not bear repeating. I saw that the speechless young officer had been joined by one of my older and more trusted comrades.

'Hang on to this one for me George, will you?' I said. 'We'll go and look for his mate.' Our burglar climbed out of the window into George's arms, and I must say he seemed more than happy to be out of the shop. I had presumed that Triton had followed me and the prisoner as he usually did, but when I turned round he was nowhere to be seen.

'Triton,' I called, 'good lad, where are you?' Nothing - which was strange. This was great, I was supposed to be searching with my dog, not for him. Then back in the shop I saw the torn wrapping off a packet of sausages, then another, and then there was my dog. He was standing in the middle of the open deep-freezer room gazing round in wonderment, with eyes as wide as a child's at Christmas, looking at the sides of meat hanging on their hooks with his tail slowly wagging. It seemed a shame to break into his reverie, but there was work to do.

'Come on son,' I said, 'let's go find them.' Triton snapped round looking guilty, then he gave a big sigh and with a last glance at the meat trotted past me to the bottom of the stairs.

He sniffed the bottom step and then bounded up them four at a time until I could hear him thundering along the upstairs landing. By the time I reached the top I was just in time to see him skid to a halt and turn right into an open doorway, his feet sliding on the bare lino as he endeavoured to change direction.

As he lunged into the room I could hear him increasing his speed as he ran round the office until there was a crash and a scream from behind the door. When I looked in I saw that Triton had got hold of the second young man by the right knee and was shaking him up and down as the youth desperately hopped about trying to retain his balance.

'There's a clever boy,' I said, 'leave him. Put him down', this last command coming too late to prevent the young man falling over backwards leaving half of the one leg of his jeans still in Triton's mouth.

'When you've finished playing with my dog,' I said, 'if it's not too much trouble you can come and join your mate downstairs and then we can charge both of you with burglary.'

'My leg hurts.' he moaned. 'And what about my jeans, look at them.'

'Frayed jeans are all the fashion nowadays aren't they?" I said, grinning.

'Not from the bloody knee down they're not' he grumbled.

No sense of humour, I thought as I took him through to the back of the shop and handed him to George, this time making sure that Triton was with me all the way. We turned the owner of the shop out of bed of course, and a little while later the butcher was most effusive in his praise when he heard the story.

'This calls for a piece of best steak,' he burbled as he disappeared into the cold room. I stood there with Triton, cheerfully anticipating a nice bit of sirloin for my grub break instead of cheese sandwiches, when the butcher returned.

'Yes, he deserves this,' he said and in front of my horrified eyes gave my lucky bloody dog about two pounds of beautiful red meat.

I forced a smile as Triton belched gently and licked his lips for the umpteenth time. He looked supremely content. Not surprising, I considered, somewhat bitterly. Two pounds of steak on top of the two pounds of sausage he had already pinched, two burglars caught and a policeman frightened half to death - he'd had a good night.

# CHAPTER TWELVE

## *INTERLUDE - A DOG HANDLER'S DAY OUT*

A report on the cultural exchange visit by the 'D' division dog section to the submarine base at HMS Dolphin, Gosport, Circa October 1990.

These are random notes compiled by the survivors of the expedition and noted by the group leader, Police Sergeant Lewis, some time after his return home.

Police Sergeant Lewis started by noting that his welcome home by his police dog was pretty friendly really, considering that dawn was breaking, but felt his dog had no right to complain about the smell of his breath when he, the dog, had voluntarily licked Police Sergeant Lewis' face. This had been in an apparent effort to revive Police Sergeant Lewis who had been lying on the kitchen floor at the time.

It was unanimously agreed that it had been a grave mistake to put Police Constable Woodall in charge of the beer kitty for the duration of the cultural evening. The resultant cries by Police Constable Woodall of 'Come on, let's go', as he completed yet another pint of lager and blackcurrant at approximately 6 ½-minute intervals will haunt other members of the party for some time.

Police Constable Walton's heroic efforts to keep up with Police Constable Woodall's rate of consumption were greatly appreciated by Police Constable Wilkinson, the group guide and social secretary and the group leader, Police Sergeant Lewis. It is hoped that when Police Constable Walton is able to leave the intensive care unit, he will once again be able to lead a full and active life. The consultant has every hope anyway, once he comes round.

Whilst on the subject of Police Constable Woodall, it was felt that his choice of lager and blackcurrant as a regular beverage should be urgently reviewed. We have received reports of mysterious staining of the urinals in at least three separate hostelries in Gosport. And what was at first thought to be an oil slick in the Solent now turns out to be harmless, and does in fact consist of pure Ribena. This may be connected with Police Constable Woodall relieving himself over the sea wall, but there is no conclusive proof.

It was agreed by the committee, that should the 'D' Division Dog Section be invited back to the submarine base in 1991, presupposing that re-building then be complete, a number of up-to-date jokes be learnt and rehearsed by each member of the party. No person will be allowed on board the Mini-bus (Note - ask Police Constable Wilkinson WHERE he has put it) until he has proved himself word-perfect on at least three different non-controversial humorous stories.

It was felt that Sergeant Lewis' joke about the Ministry of Defence Police was the best of the evening and the most well received in the actual Submariner's Club during the convivialities, but it was felt that the two-hour delay at the dock gates when leaving, while the whole party was strip-searched under armed guard, was not entirely unconnected.

It was a definite credit to Police Constable Woodall's stamina that he was able to stand and tell a joke at 9.30 p.m., indeed that he was able to stand at all, but it was thought that the choice of subject was unfortunate to say the least. The joke, involving Dracula and a number of Italian waiters, and we think, Sacha Distel, ended with the punchline, 'Drained Wops keep falling on my head'.

This was received with an appreciative silence from the audience, except for a swarthy dark man in the corner who we had thought for some time to be Police Constable Holmes changing colour again. This dark swarthy type muttered 'Mama mia, he insulta the patria', which we all took to mean that he had the wrong topping on his take-away pizza.

As we all now know, the shelling of the Isle of Wight ferry by a visiting Italian destroyer seen leaving Portsmouth at high speed about an hour later, was put down to an electronic fault in the gun room. (Note - to borrow a more comprehensive Italian-English dictionary as we can't find 'bastardos' in the one we've got).

It was agreed unanimously that we were all at a severe disadvantage at the start of the actual games challenge of the evening. We do not think that Bill, the submariner, a charming gentleman, who guided us so comprehensively round the delights of Gosport during the afternoon and early evening, meant us any deliberate harm. Rumours that he was seen chuckling later while thumbing through a pile of fivers donated by the other team captains cannot be confirmed. That our team managed to come second without too much cheating was felt to reflect great credit on our party.

It was decided by the other five perspiring members of the TLC team, that if Police Sergeant Mills (a guest from the 'C' Division Dog Section) wished to take part in the Exocet Launch' game, and further if he wished to be the 'Exocet' ever again, he would have to shed at least five stone. This could probably be achieved by routine surgery. Otherwise Police Sergeant Mills interpretation of the missile launch will continue to appear more like the launch of a potato sack down a chute, although in all fairness, the sack would have more flair.

When it comes to balancing on the board on top of a rolling pipe, it was felt that another guest, Special Constable James, fell off in the most spectacular fashion. The way the board shot off the top of the pipe, lethally hacking a swathe of destruction four inches off the ground through the ankles of the spectators, while Special Constable James went equally lethally in the other direction until he hit the wall, was thought by the uninjured spectators to be the highlight of the evening.

Police Sergeant Lewis performed the best in this particular game, actually managing to stay on the board for almost the full 15 seconds to get maximum points. It was agreed by the examining board, however, that he spoilt his performance by boringly repeating over and over again that it was because he was an ace wind-surfer that he had such superb balance.

It was felt that Police Constable Holmes' action in pushing Police Sergeant Lewis off the board in his moment of triumph was rather unfair, and he shouldn't have shouted a Hero Mutant Ninjah Turtle (Mutant Ninjah Hero Turtle?) battle cry as he did so, but it was felt that Police Constable Holmes was severely provoked as he himself cannot wind-surf and he did not see why a boring old bugger like Police Sergeant Lewis should be able to do so.

The combined H.M. Submariner/Dog Section Task Force which assembled at 1.30 a.m. with the avowed intention of taking Baghdad out had to regretfully disbanded when a couple of minor snags were discovered.

The first being that the police dogs would not fit in the torpedo tubes was easily overcome when Police Constable Holmes and Special Constable James were substituted.

The second proved more difficult. It was found that although Baghdad was surrounded by sand, the tide was not due in for about 1,000 years, depending on the greenhouse effect, and the Task Force returned to the bar for further discussions.

(Note - remember to write to HMS Dolphin soonest, to ask for Police Constable Holmes and Special Constable James to be returned before HM Submarine actually submerges).

The alternative plan was enthusiastically adopted. It was proposed that Mr. Doug Ellis be asked to invite Baghdad Rovers over for a friendly against Aston Villa. When the away supporters' coach was safely parked on the ASDA coach park, Police Constable Wilkinson and Police Constable Boots would then nip onto the coach via the emergency exit and kidnap President Saddam Hussein, while Police Sergeant Lewis was addressing the supporters in his impeccable Iraqi.

No faults could be found with this plan and it is hoped it will go ahead later this month and, therefore, bring the Gulf crisis to an end without too much bloodshed, this last depending mainly on Police Dog Shultz not having another head loss.

It was felt that should Police Constable Sly ever again attempt to sing the Police Cadet Camp song, he should be instantly garotted, and that a further paragraph be inserted into the rules limiting Police Constable Sly's time on the microphone (any microphone) to no more than 30 seconds in any one evening. No punishment was prescribed should Police Constable Sly exceed this in the future, but it was thought that a suitable one could be stipulated at the time, once we get his trousers down.

The committee decided to award a special commendation to Police Constable Boots for his sterling efforts during the latter part of the evening to chat up the oldest and ugliest woman in the room, thereby taking the pressure of everyone else.

It was noted that Police Constable Boots was very fortunate in as much that it was pension day on Thursdays in Gosport and the lady in question had to leave early as she did not want to have to wait too long at the Post Office as it tended to put too much strain on her wooden leg.

The highest award available goes to our volunteer driver, Police Sergeant Mills of the 'C' Division Dog section. Not only did he selflessly stop drinking half an hour before we were due to leave so he would be sober enough to drive, but he also accepted the varying insults, from those passengers still able to speak, about the standard of his driving, in very good part.

He was, however, particularly upset when Police Sergeant Lewis queried as to why were we going to effing Northampton instead of effing Stratford and hadn't he seen the effing sign saying 'A34 Stratford and Birmingham' at the brightly lit roundabout at the end of the Oxford by-pass (effing).

Police Sergeant Mills' explanation to the committee of enquiry, that he had been asleep since Newbury, was accepted as being totally reasonable for that hour of the morning and also that it was much prettier going via Banbury (Note - to remove Banbury Cross from meat room before next delivery of Prime Meaty Chunks).

The wimp of the year award went to Police Constable Walsh whose excuse about his wife and daughters going down with the Black Death on the previous evening was felt to be insufficient reason for his non-attendance. It was proposed by Police Constable Wilkinson, the social secretary, that if Police Constable Walsh wanted to come next year, he should pay for the whole coach and buy the first round of drinks. The committee agreed in principle that it would be fair for him to pay for the coach, but that the round of drinks would be an excessive penalty.

There were a few final thoughts of the committee before the meeting was adjourned so the members could go to the chemists, who were awaiting a further delivery of Aspirin.

It was agreed that Police Constable Walton should never have been allowed to strip down to his underpants for the boat race as it was this that probably made the beer go off. That Police Constable Woodall's valiant attempt to win the boat race by smashing a table-full of glasses instead of drinking them was foolhardy in the extreme, especially as he was barefoot at the time. That the five minutes allowed for the visit to the Submarine Museum was excessive and could be easily cut down on next year's programme.

At the mention of next year, a number of large men in white coats removed those members of the committee still breathing and there was not time to thank Police Constable Brodie for staying behind and covering the Division while everyone else was away enjoying themselves.

# CHAPTER THIRTEEN

## *CAUGHT WITH HIS TROUSERS UP*

In the Trade it's known as a 'slow cruise in'. I was in that dreamlike trance we all get into at the end of the week of nights. Although nearly six o'clock in the morning, in late June it was already broad daylight with the sun's warmth conspiring with the drone of the dog van to send me completely to sleep. Pottering along the main road which bisected my division, at a steady 27 mph was just about all I felt capable of. With only ten minutes of the shift left, bed beckoned.

The two Irishmen walking out of the front door of a shop carrying white boxes looked as surprised to see me as I was to see them. When I first glimpsed them out of the corner of my eye, my first idle thought was all to do with early morning newspaper vans and shall I stop and get a paper.

Except, Christ! - that's a shoe shop and they have just stepped through the front door frame which is devoid of glass. Now they are running off, dropping boxes everywhere. I suppose it took about half a second for my befogged brain to take in the burglary happening before my eyes and make my idle body respond.

I stamped on the brake pedal. Triton, who had been curled up peacefully in his cage, abruptly slid into the front mesh with a crash and a yelp. My brain continued to work - handbrake on, keys out, open door, shout, 'Hey you two, come here,' open back doors, grab dog, line him up, send dog.

The two men were now running away from the shattered shop windows and the pile of discarded shoe boxes. They were almost at the corner of the next side street when the one behind looked desperately over his shoulder and saw that Triton was catching up fast. Fear gave his legs extra strength and he shoved his mate hard in the back.

Whether this was to encourage him to run faster or simply to get him out of the way I don't know, but the net result was a disaster. His unbalanced partner fell flat on the pavement with a crash that made me wince. His mate leapt over him and kept running with hardly a break in pace.

'Nice friends he's got,' I thought as I reached the corner. Triton, of course, pounced on the fallen man and began to shake him vigorously by the shoulder.

Over the noise of much growling and yelling I heard a back gate slam in an entry about fifty yards further up the street. I dragged Triton off his prisoner and pointed up the road.

'Go find him' I said urgently.

Triton looked at me, looked up the empty street, looked at the man on the floor and then back at me again. I could tell what he was thinking but the last thing I needed at the moment was a smart-alec dog.

'Go on,' I shouted, 'find him.'

Triton trotted off along the pavement with his nose in the air. As he passed each entry built through the terraced houses he paused and then carried on. While Triton was searching, I had handcuffed the reluctant Irishman and helped him to his feet amongst an absolute volley of Holy Mother of Marys and Bejaysuses. Just as the cavalry arrived in the form of the local Panda car, I saw Triton turn sharply into an entry and disappear. A few seconds later a tremendous barking echoed strangely from the brick archway.

After loading our first prisoner safely in the back seat of the police car I sprinted up the street and down the alleyway where all the noise was coming from. Triton had a small middle-aged Pakistani gentleman in a night-shirt trapped in a corner of the back yard. The man was frozen stiff with fright and looked a little pale around the gills. I took hold of my dog and shut him up.

'Who the hell are you?' I said, exasperated.

'Oh, I am living here,' he said, 'I am sleeping downstairs when I hear much noise and I am coming to see what is happening. Then this dog is coming.'

'Did you see anybody?' I said.

'Oh no Sir, but I am hearing him, he is breaking my fence over there.'

The man pointed to the right hand fence beyond the outbuildings. After a brief apology to the trembling Pakistani I took Triton up the garden and put him over the fence. Triton soared effortlessly through the gap in complete contrast to my clumsy efforts to scramble over the rough and broken timbers.

Triton and I quickly searched the garden and sent through to the next. The fences were lower now and the job was much easier.

I knew from my personal radio that the adjacent street had been covered by other officers and I was hoping that it would force our man to go to ground. In what was about the sixth or seventh garden, Triton suddenly spun round as he passed the coalhouse and outside lavatory.

He carefully sniffed round the coal house door and then stood back for a second, listening carefully. He advanced to the adjacent lavatory door and stuck his nose underneath. A low growl rumbled through his body and he bit into the bottom of the door and ripped out a chunk of planking. It was a frightening example of the power of a big dog.

If there's someone in the toilet, at least he's in the right place to be frightened, I thought as I banged on the door.

'Come on out, Paddy,' I shouted and I pushed at the door but it was bolted from the inside. Fervently hoping that the occupant wasn't the householder and hard of hearing, I kicked it open.

Much to my relief the second of the shoe shop men was sat on the seat trying to look surprised. He had obviously carefully rehearsed his response should he be found.

'Jaysus,' he said, 'can't a man use his own toilet in peace, without all this banging and shouting and tings.'

'Come on out Paddy,' I said, jerking my thumb at him, 'I'm arresting you for screwing the shoe shop round the corner about ten minutes ago.'

'It wasn't me, Sorr,' he said. 'I've been in here for longer than that, Sorr, on the toilet, Sorr.'

'One slight thing Paddy,' I said, 'my mother always taught me to take my trousers down first. Didn't yours?'

He looked down and then at least had the decency to blush.

# CHAPTER FOURTEEN

## *A PRICK-LY CUSTOMER*

The old lady who flagged me down looked distressed. When I say she flagged me down, what she actually did was to throw herself in front of the dog van, frantically waving her arms. I stamped on the brakes and slid to a gravelly halt.

'What's the matter love?' I asked as I clambered out, resisting the urge to shout 'You daft old bugger.'

She gasped for breath: 'It's a man, in the bushes over there.'

She paused, gulped and went red. I didn't need to ask, but I asked anyway. 'What's he doing?'

She looked down, embarrassed, and whispered, 'He's got no trousers on and he's well…. you know.'

Yes, I did know. Flashers are a damn nuisance and, as a rule very difficult to catch. They practice their art in isolated places and normally, by the time the aggrieved woman has got to a phone, they are long gone. I was in Sutton Park, just North of Birmingham. It is not one of your run of the mill municipal parks with flowerbeds and railings and things, but a dozen or so square miles of open heath, interspersed with woodland and gorse.

With only half an hour to booking-off time, I had popped into the park to give Triton (and me) some much-needed exercise. We had had a chaotic morning, with more than half of it disappearing because of meeting about the forthcoming football season.

The end of July, and we were talking about football already, and I hate being stuck indoors. Not only that, it was payday and I hadn't had a chance to get to the bank yet, and I knew with awful certainty that I was going to be late off duty as well.

Oh well, if I can't take a joke, I shouldn't have joined.

The old lady had been really upset and I sat her down in the passenger seat of the dog van, after chucking all my junk over the back of the seat and apologetically brushing off the dog hairs. I scribbled her name and address in the back page of the vehicle log book (I wonder if the transport manager knows why his record books only last half as long as they should do), and asked her if she could describe roughly where the incident had happened. She pointed along the path near the dog van and said that he had been in the middle of a big area of holly bushes. It had taken her about 15 minutes to walk to the road, so I was guessing at about half a mile or so.

I radioed for a car to collect her from my van and take a statement, while I opened the back doors to release an impatient Triton. No one else had come down the path since the old lady, and I was hoping that he could back-track along the way she had come and hopefully lead to the scene of the dirty deed.

Mischievously I thought, 'Flashing in the middle of holly bushes sounds a bit dangerous - looks like we've got a bit of an adventurer here.'

I suppressed a grin but waved encouragingly to the old lady as we set off. Well, we almost set off. The first thing Triton did was cock his leg against a post for what seemed an eternity. I stood there feeling slightly embarrassed. When he had finally finished I cast him round on the lead.

'Good lad,' I said, 'Seek on.' And at the command, he put his nose to the ground and almost immediately picked up the scent. This time we were really off and running.

After a few hundred yards the path forked. Hesitating briefly, Triton took the left hand path and pulled me onwards. We had been together for so long by this time I didn't need to give him any more instructions and our passage through the park was almost silent. Even the thud of my size tens was completely deadened by the thick coarse grass and leaf mould carpeting the ground. Though in shirtsleeve order, I began to sweat with the exertion. Triton continued, apparently tireless, although tracking is hard work for a dog, but he nosed determinedly onwards, the thrill of the chase filling him with energy and confidence.

As we entered the plantation of holly I grew tense.   Would he still be there?

We had covered the same distance as the old lady in less than half the time, but we were about 25 minutes behind him. Triton slowed down slightly then lifted his nose from the ground and stopped.

He started sniffing the air suspiciously.   I hardly breathed.   He pulled me to the left into a clump of holly that opened out into a small clearing.   Hallelujah!   There he was!

Crouching down on the other side, girlie magazines in one hand, masturbating with the other, he was peering through a gap in the holly, no doubt looking for another victim on the parallel path.

With Triton's lead taut, we crept across the grassy clearing until we were a few feet behind him.   Triton's 'Woof' near his backside had a spectacular effect.

The flasher jumped about four feet into the air.   While in mid-air he tried to jam his fast fading willy back into his trousers, hide his magazine and zip himself up all at the same time.   He failed miserably at all three.

'You my friend,' I said, 'are nicked for indecent exposure.   Do you understand?'

He nodded morosely and for a minute or so I felt sorry for this rather inadequate youth, but not for long.   As we walked back to my van I began to chuckle to myself, so much so that our prisoner ventured to ask what I thought was so bloody funny.

'I was just thinking,' I said, 'that you could have a future in the Olympics.'

'What do you mean?' he asked sulkily.

'Well, with my dog's help you could probably win the pole vault.......without a pole.'

I think he missed the point.

# CHAPTER FIFTEEN

## *NIGHT GAMES*

'Steve's not going to like this.' These prophetic words were spoken by a probationary constable who had been attached to the dog section during the previous set of night duty. He, like me, was on his way to an alarm call at an isolated cricket club. Unlike me, however, he was the passenger in a Panda car noisily approaching the club complete with headlamps and a blue light. He uttered the words to the driver as the police car passed me on the rough track to the pavilion.

I had left the dog van 200 yards away behind a convenient hedge and was running towards the place with Triton on his lead. I had opted for this slower and quieter method of approach as I knew that the clubhouse commanded an excellent view of the drive and I never was one for giving a burglar a sporting chance.

A minute later I breathlessly joined the younger officer round the back of the building.

'Where's that prat of a driver?' I said. 'Didn't you learn anything last month?'

'I'm sorry,' said the probationer, 'he wouldn't listen to me, he's gone inside.'

'Has he indeed,' I said, 'right.'

I went to the open door and shouted, 'Police, if you don't come out I'll put the dog in.' Triton reinforced my challenge with a series of loud barks. There was a startled squawk from inside. 'No, hang on, it's me.'

Still holding Triton's lead I shouted, 'Go on son, get them.' Triton's bark dropped to a menacing growl and his claws scrabbled on the floor as he tried to get free. A frightened white face poked itself round the end of the corridor.

'It's me, it's me', it said pathetically.

'Yes, I know,' I said, 'and now I suppose you are going to tell me that our birds have flown.'

He nodded, 'There's no-one in the clubroom and the one-armed bandit has been screwed.'

I vented my frustration and anger with a pointed four-letter word and went back outside with Triton.

Tracking is not the exact science some people think, and is in fact a damn chancy business most of the time, but in this case I had no alternative as there wasn't sight or sound of our burglars. I wrestled with Triton to get his harness round his chest and then clipped the line on.

The sound of the catch snapping-to was Triton's signal to be off, and the long nylon line burnt my thumb and fingers as he accelerated away. I painfully tightened my grip on the line and slowed him down until he started to cast around in a large semi-circle. Suddenly he jack-knifed to the left and with his nose flat on the ground gave a definite pull away from the clubhouse and towards the adjacent golf course.

Once I was certain Triton was well on track I radioed through to other officers to try and cover at least some of the perimeter of the golf course and stumbled onwards at the end of the vibrating line. I could dimly see that Triton was snaking from side to side over a width of two or three yards and realized that he was probably tracking two men.

On the lush grass of one of the fairways Triton increased his speed so that I was forced to break into a jog-trot to avoid slowing him down. I was now perspiring freely and feeling most uncomfortable. The Indian take-away I had consumed an hour before was turning my stomach into a bubbling cauldron.

My radio was bouncing irritatingly against my chest in its harness and my shoes were now soaking wet from the heavy dew on the grass.

Suddenly the dark shape of my dog disappeared from view over some sort of ledge and I abruptly found myself falling into a bunker, filling my shoes full of sand. I risked a quick flash of my torch and was delighted to see another set of footprints a bit to my right. We, that is, Triton, was bang on target.

After a brief cast round at the other side of the bunker Triton once more picked up the scent and settled back into his stride. I again radioed our position and direction to the other lads on the shift but then felt the tracking line go slack as we approached one of the raised tees. Triton had lifted his nose high into the air and I could see that he was wind-scenting something. I gave him his head and he started to move to our right where I could just see the outline of a small hut built for the golfers to shelter in.

A soft growl came from Triton's throat as we approached. 'Got them,' I thought, and pulled in on the line, stopping Triton by the open entrance.

I shone my torch inside onto a couple who, while they certainly were not burglars, were definitely tasting forbidden fruits. 'What the hell are you doing here this time of night?' I said, rather unnecessarily.

'What's it bloody look like,' said the man.

'Turn your torch off,' said the girl.

Like most courting couples, she was completely naked while he was almost fully clothed.

'I'm looking for two blokes who have screwed the cricket club,' I said.

'Well, they're not in here', he said.

'Turn your torch off', said the girl.

'Have you heard anything?' I said.

'What do you bloody think', he said

'Please turn your torch off,' said the girl.

Urgent chatter started on my radio: 'There's two just come out of the hedge by the end of the pre-fabs'. That was about 400 yards in front of me. One's running down the road, one's back through the hedge onto the golf course.'

There followed further brief transmissions, mainly heavy panting noises and then a triumphant, 'Got one, got one,'

I had already left the courting couple to pick up the pieces of their ruined evening and was running hard in the direction of all the action.

'Which one you got:' I transmitted. 'The one on the road', came back immediately.

While I was fiddling with my radio, Triton stopped so abruptly that I fell over him. From my position on the ground I could see Triton's head silhouetted against the night sky. His ears were pricked high and he was listening intently to something. Then above the thudding of my heart I could hear it as well - the sound of someone running through the small copse ahead of us.

I unclipped the line from his harness. 'Go on, son,' I said, 'get him'. I should have shouted a warning really but I hadn't got time for such niceties. My curry was now making a real effort to explode from either end of my digestive tract. Falling over had been the last straw. Triton disappeared into the dark little wood and absolute silence descended.

I picked my way cautiously through the trees after him. A pigeon clattering from its roost above me made me jump but then I heard a most gratifying yell from about 80 yards to my right. A few seconds later I saw Triton had hold of our little burglar's right foot and was dragging him out of the bushes onto the edge of one of the greens.

'Good boy,' I shouted, 'leave him.' With a casual snatch of his head Triton ripped the young man's shoe off and then lay down happily gnawing it like a bone.

The youth was breathing even harder than I was and when we had both recovered a bit I said, 'Why did he bite you on the foot? He doesn't usually do that.'

'My mates all said to throw yourself flat on the deck when a dog's after you and he won't bite,' he replied, still sitting in the wet grass.

'Where on earth did they get that from?' I said.

'I think they read it in a book,' he said

'I think you had better change your reading matter,' I replied, removing the remains of his shoe from Triton's mouth. 'Try Shoe Repairing for Beginners, I think you're going to need it.'

# CHAPTER SIXTEEN

## *WHAT YOU GAIN ON THE SWINGS*

'We're going down the Castle to lift Roddy McCann.'

As briefings go it was short but very much to the point. As the six of us were all local officers we knew straight away that (a) the Castle pub was not exactly the best place in which to arrest anybody, and (b) Roddy McCann could well object very strongly to being dragged away from his pint of Guiness in mid-swallow.

When Roddy objected strongly to something, people tended to start flying round the room. He was a big lad and not renowned for his love of policemen. In fact he was not renowned for his love of anybody. Even Mary, his long suffering common law wife, had recently packed her bags after sticking loyally by him through the years. She had provided him with alibi after alibi, invariably being rewarded with a black eye or split lip for her pains.

The last time however, Roddy had hit her either too hard or once too often and she had gone. Roddy pretended not to care. 'Good riddance to the slut', was his usual comment, but it was noticed that he had become even more wayward and violent in the past few weeks.

It had all culminated in the vicious beating of a prostitute he had gone with a couple of nights before. Not satisfied with the standard of service offered, instead of bouncing her on the bed he started bouncing her round the walls instead. When her minder tried to intervene he was promptly despatched through the bedroom window, which was closed, and ended up in the road-works beneath, which were open.

All in all the pair of them were not very well, and although we didn't shed many tears for the minder, his enforced flight being the source of much canteen hilarity for weeks afterwards, we actually had two statements of complaint. So Roddy McCann was coming in.

'Steve, I don't want you and your growler inside the pub unless the wheel falls off. Not after last time.' I grinned at Fred, the DC organizing the raid. I bet you keep well clear of Triton tonight, I thought, remembering how Triton had nailed him in the thigh when Fred had got too close in the middle of the last punch-up we had with a prisoner. Triton was not over fussy when aroused.

'If you park up opposite and stand by,' Fred continued, 'we'll give you a shout on the air if Roddy cuts up, and if you do have to come inside, keep that bloody dog away from my bloody arse, okay?'

'Okay Fred' I said, rolling my eyes, and this time everybody grinned.

We finished our teas and Pete, the local beat officer, and I squeezed into my dark blue Mini-van I had left parked outside Edward Road nick. Triton sat up in his cage behind me and had a good sniff of Pete through the mesh. Having decided it was alright for Pete to be in his dog van he lay down again with no more than a minor grumble.

I watched the four detectives climb into Fred's Granada and as it moved away from the kerb I followed. Triton sat up again and in the rear view mirror I could see his face staring intently through the windscreen. I always wondered if he didn't trust my driving or whether he was just nosey.

It was less than a mile to the Castle and when I saw Fred swing his car into the side car park I pulled the dog van into the opposite kerb. I switched off the engine and the lights and Pete and I took off our caps and waited.

I looped my lead in my right hand so the catch was between my finger and thumb. There was a reason for this. When I opened the back doors to let Triton out, he usually came out fast and sneaky and I had to grab him first time or all was lost.

Pete tapped his radio, then squeezed it in the middle and finally held it to his ear to see if it was ticking. 'It's bloody quiet,' he said. "Is yours working?' Just then a routine transmission saved me the trouble of replying. 'Knowing the CID, they're probably having a pint first', I said. It was only two minutes since they had gone in, but it seemed longer.

We had a good view of the front of the pub and as we watched impatiently a tall West Indian appeared in the doorway and carefully looked around. Pete and I shrank back further in our seats. 'That's Junior Marquesa' said Pete, 'What's he up to?'

Apparently satisfied that he was unobserved, Junior loped down the steps and, removing a package from inside his jacket, secreted it between the pub wall and a drainpipe. He straightened up and after another glance over the car park he took the six steps in two strides and disappeared back inside.

'He thinks Fred and the lads are Drug Squad', I said to Pete. 'We'll have him when he comes out and collects. You go left and I'll go right but wait till he picks it up.'

There was no way Pete or I could get near the Castle in uniform without being spotted, so we were forced to sit and wait in our anonymous little Mini-van. Just then the four CID men appeared at the side door with a very subdued Roddy McCann, and with a quick thumbs-up to us they climbed into their car and shot off. 'Well, that's the big problem solved,' I said to Pete. 'Now for Junior.'

Right on cue Junior re-appeared in the doorway and with a smile of satisfaction watched the CID car out of sight. Confident now, he strolled over to the drainpipe and as soon as his back was turned Pete and I rolled out of the van.

As I scuttled to the back doors to get Triton out, Pete went forward crouching below the level of the parked cars until he could get an opportunity to cross the road. I grabbed Triton as he launched himself from the van and clipped his lead on. Junior was still crouched by the drainpipe so I started across the road, angling to the right to come round behind him. Then it all went wrong.

A car started up in the car park and as it swung round its headlights picked out first Junior, who jumped to his feet, and then me and Triton who were now brightly illuminated in the middle of the road. Junior saw us and started to run, not back into the Castle, thank God, where he might have made it through the bar, but across the front car park towards Pete.

Triton was doing his best to tear my left arm out of its socket as I shouted, 'Hold it Junior, or the dog will have you.' with Triton indicating with a barrage of noise that he was just the dog to do it. As I tried to release the lead I heard Pete shout, 'Alright, Steve. I've got him', and I saw Pete appear from between two parked cars and block the pavement.

Without breaking his stride, Junior jumped onto the boot of one of them, over the roof, down the bonnet and into the road, now giving Triton a clear run. I was just about to let him go when Pete came tearing across the road shouting, 'You effing bastard, I'll bloody have you.'

'Pete,' I shouted, 'get out of the bloody way.' But Pete was having his own private head loss by now and I was forced to watch the pair of them disappear down a side street. Fuming, I threw a protesting Triton back into the dog van and we screamed off round the corner in time to see them swerve to the right into a children's playground. I could see that Pete was slowing down and I drove past him, recklessly squeezing the van between the swings and a concoction of concrete pipes until I could see Junior again.

'This time, son,' I said to Triton, 'he's definitely yours.' Mercifully I stopped the van just on the edge of the unseen sand pit. I tore open the back doors and away went Triton, determined to vent his frustration on Junior, who was very co-operatively running along the van's headlight beams. It was a close thing even so.

Triton caught up with him just as he reached the six-foot wall at the far side of the playground. Junior jumped for the top and actually got his body and one leg onto the wall, but had left the other hanging down as he tried to force himself over.

Triton leapt for the leg and dug his teeth deep into the calf muscle. When he started pulling down with all his strength Junior first questioned Triton's parentage and then mine as I joined in the tug-of-war a few seconds later.

Something had to give way and it was not going to be Triton, that was for sure. He was growling right down in his throat, with a look of utter determination on his face, as Junior slowly but surely lost his grip and started to come down our side. It ended in a rush as Junior suddenly let go and ended up in a cursing heap at the bottom.

'Leave him, son,' I said to Triton. 'LEAVE HIM,' and at the shouted command he disentangled himself from Junior's leg and shredded trousers. 'NO,' I shouted as Triton spun round as Pete came jogging up to us. 'Although,' I said to Pete, 'I'm bloody tempted.'

'Sorry, Steve,' said Pete, 'I thought I could get him. Forgot about the dog.' 'Make sure you remember next time,' I said, 'or Triton will have to remind you.'

I turned to Junior, 'Not your lucky day really. We weren't after you at all. We only went to the Castle for Roddy McCann.'

Junior raised his eyes to heaven, 'Not after me he says.' He looked down pointedly at his leg. 'Jesus Christ man. What's that hell hound of yours going to do when you ARE after me?'

'That,' I said to Junior, 'is something for us all to look forward to.'

I looked down at Triton and could have sworn that he nodded his head.

# CHAPTER SEVENTEEN

## *HAPPY HOLIDAY*

The last day before you go on annual leave is always a time that is fraught with tension. Rule number one, of course, is not to get involved with anything that could possibly delay your long-awaited departure to the coast. For better or worse we had decided to try camping this particular year. My ancient estate car was already groaning with the weight of a borrowed frame tent and sleeping bags perched on the roof rack.

The load space, normally Police Dog Triton's little kingdom, was packed solid with all the junk apparently necessary for two adults and three young boys to survive under canvas for two weeks. Because of this Triton was due to spend his first holiday in the kennels. I had not dared tell him yet. I thought I'd better break it to him gently when I took him there later in the afternoon.

I had managed to swap my evening shift for a day shift and was looking forward to keeping out of trouble for the next seven hours. All went well up to lunch time. It had been a quiet Friday until at about half past two my personal radio crackled into life, 'Lady at 37 Greenway Road has returned home and can't open the front door. Thinks it has been bolted from the inside.'

ETA three minutes,' I replied while thinking vile thoughts. I didn't really want a prisoner at this late stage but nevertheless I thrashed the dog van along the side streets of Kings Health and arrived at the same time as Dave, a local DC. While he covered the front of the house, I ran round the back with Triton.

The kitchen door was open and I cautiously went inside. I always kept Triton on the lead when searching houses as his boundless enthusiasm for the job usually translated itself into accidentally wrecking the place. We quickly completed the ground floor and I indicated to Dave through the front window that we were going upstairs.

We were at the turn of the staircase when Triton suddenly stopped and swung his head round to the right. He raised his nose slightly and carefully sniffed the air. After a couple of seconds' deep thought, he slowly and deliberately moved forward onto the landing and pulled me towards the main bedroom, increasing his speed as we went. The door was almost shut but Triton rammed his nose in the slit and shouldered it open slamming it back against the dresser.

I managed to halt his onward rush as he reached the bed because I could see by then that the object of his attention was not in any position to make a run for it. Our burglar was in a deep sleep, curled up comfortably on top of the bedclothes making gentle snoring noises. Triton cocked his head to one side and looked at him puzzled. The man's comatose state was easily explained by the empty bottle of expensive malt whisky lying on the bedclothes by his limp right hand.

I went to the window and opened it. 'Dave, come up here and look at this,' I called down.

'Well, well, sleeping beauty himself,' Dave laughed when he joined me. 'Are you going to be the handsome prince and give him a big kiss to wake him up?'

'Not me,' I said. 'But it's time he had an alarm call.' I took a tight grip on Triton's lead and took him towards the bed until he was almost nose to nose with the slumbering occupant.

'Good lad,' I said to Triton, 'SPEAK'. The resulting 'woof' was loud enough to wake the dead, and it did. His eyes shot open with incomprehension turning to sheer terror and instant sobriety.

'What the hell, what the bloody hell, oh my God', was the best he could do as he jerked violently upright into the sitting position. From there he saw me and Dave grinning at him and he collapsed back onto the pillow muttering, 'Bastards, oh you bastards.'

'Got a drink problem have we, mate?' said Dave solicitously.

'Jesus, it's not funny,' said our sleepy head, but in spite of himself he started to smile. 'What a prat, what a stupid prat. Take me away I deserve it.'

Dave collected the empty bottle and a bag full of property he found in another bedroom and I took Chummy back to Kings Heath nick.

There the poor lad had to suffer even more as all the obvious jokes were thrown at him.

'What's the charge Steve?' said Mac the Office Sergeant. 'Drunk in charge of house-breaking implements or driving a bed under the influence?'

With everybody staring at our unfortunate man and laughing, I could see his patience was wearing thin and he was quite pleased when Dave took him up to the CID Office for interview. Knowing that I was going on annual leave Dave had offered to deal with him and I was able to leave Kings Heath in perfect time to take Triton to the kennels and be able to book off duty.

I shut Triton in the kennel block and fondled his head through the bars. He looked at me reproachfully.

'I'll be back soon son,' I said, lying through my back teeth. 'Honest, it won't be long'. I stood up, and Triton went and lay on his bed board looking disconsolate.

'Look after him for me Jan, won't you,' I said to the kennel maid.

'Oh stop worrying,' she replied. 'They're all the same until you've gone, he'll be bright as ninepence in the morning'.

'Ta ra son,' I said to Triton and, as if in reply, he tucked his nose in under his tail and looked up at me sadly. I went.

In the chaos of our departure for Devon all thoughts of drunken burglars and lonely dogs were banished from my mind. Jamming three excited small boys into the back seat amidst even more luggage and easing my way onto the crowded M5 motorway was more than enough to occupy my thoughts. But with no more than a bit of plug trouble, my old Vauxhall eventually made it to the camp site.

The weather was kind to us and after a few blissful sunny days I had completely switched off from the Police Force and became immersed in such intractable problems as to how long would the money last if I bought five ice-creams three times a day for twelve days.

I missed Triton of course but I assured myself that he would be alright.

Meanwhile, back at the kennels all was not well. On the Wednesday, while Triton was being exercised, he got into a fight with another police dog and together they disappeared off over the fields with the kennel maids being left far behind. The second dog turned up back at the kennels ten minutes later, but Triton was gone. He didn't like the place and the fight was obviously the last straw. He was off in search of his home comforts.

An urgent search got under way but there was no trace of him. Then, about three hours later and five miles away, a probationary constable in Kings Heath High Street was a bit perturbed when a large dog came and sat next to him.

The standard reaction to this situation 'Go on, sod off you big mutt' did not work, and worse still, the dog insisted on following him wherever he went. So it caused considerable consternation amongst the front office staff at Kings Heath when this large dog padded in after the young officer and plonked himself down under the charge desk. The look in the dog's eyes when approached kept all at bay and most of the work ground to a halt while it was decided what to do.

Fortunately fate intervened and Dave, the detective we had been involved with a few days before, wandered into the office.

'Surely that's Steve's dog,' he said. 'Come here Triton, what's the matter?'

Triton wearily got to his feet and nuzzled Dave's hand. A quick check of the teleprinter messages still on the machine confirmed what had happened and soon Triton was on his way back to captivity. He bid for freedom had taken him across four main roads. He had found his way through five miles of congested suburbs and attached himself to a police officer not far from my parade station. Not bad.

I went to collect him as soon as we returned from our holidays. He was obviously delighted to see me. His welcome when I opened the kennel door was overwhelming. He completely ruined my shirt by jumping up all over me, licked my face clean and nearly knocked me silly when the top of his head caught me under the chin. When he calmed down I put his lead on and took him for a walk. I met Jan coming back with another dog.

'Has he behaved himself?' I asked.

'Well', said Jan, 'It's funny you should ask, but...'

# CHAPTER EIGHTEEN

## *A CLEAN BREAK*

The day before I got promoted, I broke my leg. Nothing very heroic. Just playing rugby again. Most of my missing teeth and various other damaged bits and pieces are as a direct result of playing in the front row of the scrum over a period of thirty years or so. I'm refereeing now, in my old age, having exchanged physical abuse for verbal. My wife thinks the description of my position on the field of play as 'loose head prop' was very appropriate, but she never did appreciate the importance of rugby and Camp Hill Rugby Club.

It had been a Sunday afternoon cup match away, and after I had been discharged from Kidderminster Hospital, still in my rugby kit and still covered in mud, I got a lift home and hobbled into the house on my nice new crutches. Triton padded down the hall and sniffed suspiciously at the shiny white plaster encasing the lower half of my left leg. He looked at me. 'What have you done now, you daft bugger,' he seemed to say. I could only shrug my shoulders at him and hopped into the living room preparatory to flopping down on the settee.

'Oh no you don't,' came a different voice. 'You can get all that mud off first before you touch anything. Bathroom!'

Feeling like a naughty eight-year-old, I laboriously mounted the stairs using my backside and right leg to shuffle up backwards. A few minutes later I sat in the shower tray with my left leg stuck out through the curtains, trying to scrub off the caked mud and gloomily wondering what idiot had voiced the opinion that there is a nurse in every woman. Ha!

Going downstairs is easier, you just slide down until you hit the bottom. Ouch! By now I was exhausted; it had not been a good day. Triton sat by the front door looking expectant. God, he wanted to go for a walk.

'Forget it' I snapped at him. His ears drooped, his tail stilled. I looked helplessly at him. 'Oh alright, just up the road then,' I said, and 'Mind my bloody leg' as he started to jump about.

Life on crutches is not easy. I wrapped Triton's lead round my left wrist and started off slowly along the pavement, fervently hoping he didn't meet next door's cat. I had no wish to zoom down the road like something out of a Tom and Jerry cartoon.

The next morning, Monday, I phoned the Chief Superintendent's secretary on the Division to which I had been promoted. 'Yes', I said, 'this is Sergeant Lewis. I've just been promoted to your Division and I have an appointment to see the Chief Superintendent at 10. o'clock.'

'Oh yes,' said the pleasant voice at the other end. 'It is in his diary and he is looking forward to meeting you.'

'Well,' I said, 'I'm afraid there is a slight snag,' and I went on to explain what had happened.

There was a strangled cry down the phone, obviously someone else's opinion of dog handlers and rugby players had just been confirmed.

The business of the day over I struggled down the road with Triton again, not so difficult this time, but crutches are definitely an acquired taste. Right - dog walked, wife at work, kids at school. Time for breakfast. Cup of coffee, do the crossword and, yes, I think a fried egg sandwich will go down well. Nobody in to tell me it's bad for me, so here we go.

Boiling the kettle and frying the eggs is no problem, I'm going to enjoy this. Coffee is in the mug, sandwich is on the plate. So here we go, into the front room with the paper for a leisurely breakfast. Except we don't.

How the hell do you carry a cup of coffee or a plate while holding yourself upright on crutches? I tried, but it was impossible, and I was reduced to eating and drinking in a strictly upright manner in the kitchen. Triton watched me, looking distinctly amused. Life on crutches is definitely not easy.

Fortunately for the human race, and rugby players, broken bones do heal, and within six weeks or so I was gingerly using my left leg again.

I started taking Triton for long walks to build up both my fitness and his, and the fine autumn days passed pleasantly enough.

On one longish round trip I decided to pop into my bank to make an appointment to see the manager. We were in dire need of a bit of an overdraft. Three fast growing boys, two ancient cars and a small extension to the garage were stretching the budget just a touch.

A couple of hundred pounds extra would do very nicely. I leaned through the enquiry window and explained my mission to the young lady.

'I think he can see you now,' she said. 'He's free all this morning.'

'Oh,' I said. 'I didn't expect to see him his morning, I've got my dog with me and I'm hardly dressed for the part.'

'Don't worry,' she said. 'I'll explain and he's quite human really. He won't mind'.

A few minutes later I walked into the manager's office with Triton. Before I could say a word the manager held his arms up in mock surrender, "You can have it" he said. 'Anything you want, just take it'.

I grinned at him, he grinned back.

I liked this man.

'How's your leg?' he said. 'I read about it in the local rag'. Within minutes I was drinking a very pleasant cup of coffee and Triton was being personally fed digestive biscuits by the manager's very attractive secretary. I wish she'd fondle my ears like that.

Sure enough, when the biscuits were all gone he rolled over onto his back to have his tummy rubbed. Tongue lolling, eyes rolling, he looked up at me in a peculiar upside-down way while the secretary stroked his chest. Any thoughts between us were superfluous, he was a lucky devil and he knew it. But he had just got me the easiest bank loan I'll ever have.

# CHAPTER NINETEEN

## *FOXY LADY IN DISTRESS*

'Ah, Dog Men, just the very people I need.' Inspector Bernie Morris was all joviality. Tom and I recognized the signs.

Without pausing we smartly about turned and began to hurriedly exit from the canteen.

'Stand fast there, stand fast I say', stopped us in our tracks.

Tom and I looked round as if surprised.

'You want us, Sir?' I enquired innocently.

'Yes Sarge, I do. What do you know about foxes?'

'Foxes, Sir?' I replied. 'Well they're kind of reddy brown with pointy ears and a cute bushy tail.'

The Inspector's eyebrows shot up.

'I know all that,' he said impatiently. 'Now I've got a little job for you which will greatly improve your knowledge of Monsieur Renard. There is a kind lady in Four Oaks who is worried about a fox that is in her back garden. She thinks it is ill.'

'But we handle dogs not foxes,' I protested. 'Can't the RSPCA help?'

'They've got no one available,' he replied, 'and I'm delegating you two. Dogs, foxes, they're all the same. Go and deal with it.'

'But,' I said.

'Go,' he said.

We went.

Tom and I cruised thoughtfully up to the Four Oaks area. Police dogs Triton and Czar continued their noisy efforts to get at each other by chewing through the partition in the back of the dog van.

Occasional shouts of 'SHUT UP' and 'GET DOWN' punctuated our passage through the smart residential area until we arrived at the address we had been given.

We were shown through to the spacious rear garden by a lady who was indeed kindly. 'I'm sorry to trouble you' and 'Thank you for coming' were a definite improvement on some of the welcomes we had received over the years. And then there was our fox. He was old and grey muzzled, and was lying awkwardly on the frosty grass as if his rear end was stuck to the ground.

'Looks like he's been hit by a car and dragged himself here,' Tom said, 'I don't think he can move any further'.

We went a bit closer to be greeted by a head movement as quick as a striking snake and a snapping mouthful of yellow teeth. We hastily retreated a few yards and looked afresh at our problem. He regarded us with a baleful glare over a wide open mouth and made hissing noises.

'I think he will have to be put out of his misery,' I said. 'The trouble is, how are we going to do it?'

'We could try our vet,' Tom said.

'It's Sunday afternoon,' I replied, 'he'll probably be playing golf. If we fetched him off the course he would club us with his eight iron, never mind the fox.'

The Lady of the house came out with two cups of tea. Visibly distressed at the state of the fox, she said, 'The poor think really ought to be put down, can't you get a gun or something?'

I started to shake my head but then my eyes met Tom's over the rim of my cup.

'How about Sid', he said, putting my thought into words.

Sid was a farmer on the boundary of our division. He was the very antithesis to nature preservation. Any animal or bird which dared stray onto his land or into his air space saw him reaching for his twelve-bore.

We often used his fields to train our dogs for tracking and searching, and we had grown quite used to the shattering blast of Sid's shot-gun as another errant rabbit bit the dust.

Tom and I gulped our tea down, and after explaining to our host we set off to Sid's farm. Sid's eyes gleamed at the thought of a fox to kill, but he shook his head.

'I'd love to help you lads,' he said somewhat sorrowfully, 'but I'm just starting milking. I'll be ages yet. Tell you what, though, you can borrow my gun'.

I looked at Tom doubtfully. Being city lads, to us shot-guns were weapons which came sawn-off and were usually associated with stocking masks and similar paraphernalia. I shrugged my shoulders, there was no alternative, an animal was needlessly suffering and a nice lady was upset.

'Okay, you're on,' I said to Sid, and a few minutes later we were hurrying back complete with shotgun and a pocketful of cartridges.

'Before we do this, love,' I began, but she held up her hand to silence me.

'Don't worry,' she said, 'I'm a nurse, and we have to do a lot of things we're not supposed to as well. I just want the poor creature free from pain. 'Go ahead.'

'If I ever break a leg,' I said, 'remind me not to come to your hospital.'

She smiled. 'As we only shoot people with two broken legs, you'd be alright.'

I loaded the shotgun and took aim. The 'BOOM' of the discharge echoed round the garden and sent magpies screaming from the poplar trees. The coal shovel and a black plastic dustbin liner tidied things up and a short while later we left to return the gun to Sid.

Inspector Morris was still in jovial mood when he greeted us back at the nick.

'It's our two intrepid explorers returned from the wilds. And how did the fox hunt go?'

'Okay Sir, thanks,' I said. Adding non-commitally, 'we solved the lady's problem'.

'Good, good,' he said half turning to go, then he stopped. There must have been something in our attitude which made his nerve endings twitch.

'Tell me,' he said, 'HOW did you solve her problem?'

I looked at him steadily, 'We borrowed a gun and shot it.'

The Inspector's lips silently mouthed my words, then he started to smile, then he stopped smiling and said out loud, 'You did borrow a gun and shoot it - didn't you?' I had watched the expression on his face go from doubt to disbelief and on to certainty.

'Yes sir,' I said cheerfully, 'we nipped up to Sid's farm and.. ...'

'Stop,' he said, 'I don't want to know.' Do you understand, Sergeant, 'I DON'T WANT TO KNOW.'

He turned and retreated down the corridor as if we had the plague.

'Do you want a duty report, Sir?' I called after him.

He turned towards us looking quite pale.

'No. I do not want a duty report or any other kind of report... IS THAT CLEAR?'

Tom and I were grinning but it did not seem to make him any happier. It may be coincidence but nobody has asked us to deal with an injured fox since.

# CHAPTER TWENTY

## *TRITON'S LAST PRISONER (ALMOST)*

In a dark side street in Nechells, an Inner city area of Birmingham, a fellow sergeant of mine, Mike Davies, was intrigued by a car with a man and a woman inside. They were not performing as a courting couple, just sitting upright in the front seats, not even talking to each other. When he had driven past them they had not looked at him, just stared straight ahead unmoving.

Mike checked the number with the controller - not reported stolen. Owner lived on the other side of the city. He was about to shrug his shoulders and leave it, but then thought 'What the hell, I'll give it a spin. You never know'. That's the whole thing about the Police Force, you never know. So you have to ask, especially at 2.00 a.m.

He pulled his car round behind the other and went to the driver's door. 'Alright mate?' Mike said through the window.

'Yes thank you, officer,' said the driver politely. 'We were just chatting, no problem is there?'

'No, no problem,' said Mike. 'Your car is it?'

'No, it's my wife's brother's actually, we've just borrowed it for the evening'.

Mike was just a fraction of a second late in feeling the presence of a third person behind him. The driver's story of it being his wife's brother's car had begun to arouse his suspicions that all was not well. The reply was just the sort of garbage we are used to hearing as a hastily thought-up cover story.

The car was parked on the off-side of the road alongside a narrow pavement. What Mike hadn't noticed in the dark was an open gateway in the high wall surrounding the churchyard behind him.

As he began to turn he felt a tremendous blow in his kidneys. At the same time the driver slammed the car door open, catching him in the knees and chest and knocking him backwards onto the pavement.

Mike was mad, bloody mad. He was still gripping his radio in his right hand and pressed the button shouting 'Assistance, Church Road' twice, as the second man came at him again. He ducked a flying boot and grabbed the leg, dropping his radio as he did so, and hung on, pulling the man off balance.

He heard the car engine start, the driver shouting to his mate, 'For Christ's sake come on or we're dead'.

The man dragged his leg from Mike's grasp and ran to the revving car. Mike was now really bloody mad. He had what is known in the trade as a head loss, and scrambling to his feet he dived in through the open driver's window as the car started to move off. With his legs hanging outside the car he started wrestling with the driver, ignoring the blows being rained on him by the two passengers. You could say that the driver's concentration was being impaired, especially when his mate missed Mike's head altogether and caught him a tidy bang behind his left ear.

The car veered across the road out of control and slammed under the rear of a parked lorry. The impact temporarily stunned all the occupants and Mike fell out, spitting blood and teeth. He was now really bloody mad.

I was just about to augment the housekeeping with my best hand of the night in the canteen at Aston, when Mike's assistance call came over the air. It was just about changeover time for the two meal breaks and well over half the night shift was in the room, either thoughtfully digesting, or about to savour the delights of the various local take-aways.

There was a mass frantic exit through the doorway and a mad gallop down the stairs and out into the yard. I had a slight advantage here.

I always reversed the dog van into its parking space when I visited the nick for any reason, so all I had to do was pick the keys up from the floor, jam them in the ignition and I was away. The watch Inspector wrenched open my passenger door and threw himself into the seat as I moved off, trying to make himself comfortable amongst the litter of wellington boots and my bag full of dog handlers' junk that was strewn over the passenger side.

Triton started barking loudly in the back of the van, making the gaffer jump and bang his head on the roof. He had time to mutter 'Jesus Christ' at Triton, but then became more concerned with hanging on as I slammed out of the back gateway of the nick and executed a screaming left turn as I accelerated hard. We had a mile and a half to go.

Once on the main road I worked the dog van up to over seventy, only to have the fast response car overtake us like we were standing still. A few seconds later I saw him start braking hard as he prepared to take the right turn towards Church Road. Triton jammed himself against the front of the cage as I followed the other police car into its chassis-twisting turn. My front suspension bottomed out on the other side of the canal bridge but nothing broke, and with a fast left-hander we were into the street leading to Church Road.

The gaffer saw him first. We had no description to go on of course, but anyone running like that has got to be fair game. He ran out of a side alley on our right, between us and the fast response car, now almost 200 yards in front.

'That's the bastard, Steve', shouted the gaffer just as Triton started a frantic barking as he saw him in my headlight beams. Our quarry zipped across the road in a split second and disappeared up the opposite alley on our left.

By now I was standing the dog van on its nose in the four-wheel dry skid. I jerked the hand brake on as the van finally stopped and scrambled out to release Triton.

The Inspector wisely stayed in the van for a couple of seconds, he'd seen dog men work before. No time for a challenge or other such boring technicalities. 'Go on son, get him' I shouted, as Triton rocketed out of the back doors and legged it up the entry.

He was now over ten years old and approaching retirement, but with the excitement of the chase was giving a fair impression of a two-year-old greyhound.

He disappeared into the darkness and the night became full of sounds. A dustbin clattered over. A back gate crashed open. A pile of milk bottles went.

All this was to my left and I took a narrower alleyway in that direction. At the end a gate was swinging and I charged through it followed by the Inspector. He cannoned into my back as I stopped to listen. Nothing. Then I heard a scrambling of feet on a fence about three gardens away, immediately followed by a low growl and a scream. With the gaffer following I jumped over the low chestnut fencing between the gardens, towards the screams. An unseen clothes line cleanly took my cap off my head in the second garden. It could have been worse, it could have been lower; but no time for such thoughts.

The gaffer's torch revealed Chummy lying flat on his face yelling his head off. He had a good excuse for this unseemly behaviour. Triton had a full mouthful at the top of his left thigh and his teeth were obviously digging deep. He had caught him as he was trying to scramble over the higher six-foot panel fence at the far side of this garden, bitten him on the leg and dragged him off.

'Good lad', I yelled, 'clever boy'.

'Gerrhimoff my bloody leg' screamed our prisoner, who was none too happy at my complimenting Triton, whose growling now sounded more akin to a happy purring.

I grabbed Triton's choke chain and at this he carefully disengaged his teeth from amongst the muscle and torn denim and stood there panting with a very smug look on his face.

'That was bloody great, Steve', said the gaffer as he dragged our friend to his feet. 'Now let's find out what he's done'.

We handcuffed him and retraced our steps to the dog van. A quick radio message saw our prisoner safely ensconced in the back of a police car, and we carried on to Church Road.

Most of the loose ends had been tied up when we got there. Mike, the sergeant who had started it all, had successfully managed to detain the driver. The female passenger had been knocked half unconscious by the impact with the lorry and was on her way to hospital under escort. A search of the churchyard had revealed that they had been breaking into the adjacent factory premises via the fire escape which ended down by the side wall of the church hall.

Then a message came over the radio from one of the Panda men. He had found an unlocked pick-up truck parked in the next side street.

'That's more like it', said the gaffer. 'It was obviously brass and copper they were after. They wouldn't get much in that car. I wonder if there's another one', he mused, 'it would make sense, two in the car and two in the pick-up. Probably long gone by now, but we'll give it a try. Can you do the churchyard please, Steve'.

Triton picked his way carefully through the long grass and undergrowth. The graves were long neglected and many of the head stones were standing at crazy angles. Some of the graves themselves had sunk below ground level for a foot or so and I was not finding the search easy.

I have not normally got the most vivid imagination, but it was beginning to work overtime. I'd seen enough horror films and I just knew what went on in graveyards in the early hours. It usually involved one of Dracula's mates, and lots of blood and screaming.

Even though there was a reasonable backwash from the street lights and I had my torch and my dog, I was still getting the heeby-jeebies a bit as we struggled up towards the church.

By the time we got there Triton was tired and I was knackered. I sat down at the top of the three steps on the path leading to the vicarage. Triton lay down at my feet and sighed as he put his head on his front paws. I leaned forward and fondled his ears, 'Are you alright, old fellah?' I said softly. Triton pulled his head up and nuzzled my hand.

Suddenly he jerked his head back and looked intently behind me. As I turned my head round I heard a soft sound behind me and found myself looking up at what appeared to be the biggest Great Dane in the world, about the size of the Hound of the Baskervilles.

Much to my credit, I didn't scream but held Triton by the scruff of the neck and slowly, oh so slowly, rose to my feet. From where I was now standing at the bottom of the short flight of steps my eyes were at least level with the Dane's.

A deep voice from the darkness called 'What's going on?' It was the vicar, the bloody vicar and his bloody dog.

'It's the police', I squeaked.

'Oh, I see' said the vicar. 'Come here, Henry'.

Henry turned and obediently trotted, like a small pony, back to his owner's side. My heart stopped trying to hammer its way out of my rib-cage and after a few deep breaths I stammered out an explanation of our presence. After a brief chat the vicar returned to his bed, taking Henry with him, leaving me standing there feeling absolutely drained.

The overwhelming temptation was to knock it on the head there and then, go back to the van and go in for a cuppa, but we had already done about two-thirds of the churchyard and the last bit was downhill, so off we went again.

Although our hearts weren't really in it, we made a fair effort at the search until we were almost down to the gate again. Just as I was about to call Triton to me, I saw him hesitate and sniff the air. 'What you got, son', I said.

He turned away and carefully groped his way towards a large bush. He stopped at the edge and moved a few feet to his left and then stuck his nose in through the branches.

Obviously not wishing to expend any unnecessary energy, Triton gave out a single short bark and then turned to look at me. I almost laughed at the expression on his face. He was telling me that he had found someone who was proving difficult to get at and would I please help. I love old dogs.

I went to the bush, which was rather like a wild tree with its trunk and all the foliage at ground level, and about 30 feet in diameter. I forced my way through the branches, shining my torch all over the place, but could see nothing. I tried bluff. 'All right, you come on out, you're nicked', I shouted into the darkness. There was no response.

'Are you OK, Steve,' called the gaffer from the church gate.

'Yes I think so,' I replied. 'I'm pretty sure our friend is in here somewhere, it's just sorting out where'.

'Do you want the lads to help?' he said.

'Hang on a minute,' I shouted back, 'I'll give the dog another go.'

This last sentence was as much for the benefit of anybody in the bush as for the gaffer, but I parted some of the lower branches and called Triton in. He squeezed through and started unsteadily clambering over the lower branches with his legs straddled all over the place and his nose going like that of a suspicious hamster.

About half way across he burrowed his head downwards through the leaves until there was a shout, 'OK, OK. I give in now. He's got my shoulder'.

Too late mate, I thought as I balanced on the branches trying to get to them. Triton's body was jerking almost convulsively as he dragged his man out and, sure enough, first a shoulder appeared and then a head, with a terrified face attached. I called Triton off at this point, and he stood there nose to nose with his client, daring him to blink. He didn't. Two of the lads off the shift pulled number four from his hidey-hole and we all returned to the nick in triumph.

Much later, with all the documentation and interviews completed, we all gathered back in the canteen while the youngest probationary constable made a huge pot of tea with the Inspector's 'And it had better be better than the last one you made,' ringing in his ears.

Triton padded round the room scrounging sweet-and-sour pork balls (Cantonese style), prawn crackers and various other bits of mostly unwanted, re-heated curries. God knows what his stomach would be like the next day. I'd probably have to leave the van windows open, but it would be a small price to pay. For an old bugger he'd done well, and he knew it.

He came over to me and laid his chin on my thigh, his eyes looked into mine and said 'How was that boss?'

'Pretty good, son,' I said, 'pretty good'.

# CHAPTER TWENTY ONE

## *STILL THE BOSS*

Some nine months before Triton retired from active work, I went to our kennels to view his prospective replacement. I took Ann and my three sons with me, or to be more accurate, they all insisted on coming and I had no choice in the matter.

We walked down the kennel block and I eyed rather dubiously and critically the litter of three twelve-week-old puppies playing together behind the bars. There didn't seem much to choose between them, except one did seem livelier and, 'Dad, he's got the biggest feet, Dad', and Dad he's got dark brown eyes like Triton, Dad'. Ann looked at me, 'Well, what shall we call him:' A decision had obviously been made, so out came he of the big feet and we all piled into my battered estate car.

From his lordly position in the rear, Triton stood up and suspiciously sniffed the air at the interloper who was sitting on the floor between Ann's feet and the front. I reached back and tickled Triton on the forehead. 'It's alright, son,' I said, he's only a pup'. Less than five minutes and two miles later the 'pup' deposited his dinner over Ann's shoes. It was to be the first of many such excitements.

After a protracted family discussion that evening the newcomer was finally named 'Sonny'. Not as majestic or dignified as 'Triton', I agree, but how can you give a dignified name to a little fat bundle of fur and fluff with floppy ears.

I continued to work with Triton, of course, although he was by now past his tenth birthday. This was well over the average age of a police dog's retirement which is usually about nine years old.

He had had just a little trouble jumping over fences in the last 12 months, but as long as I was still strong enough to lift him and help him over, we managed.

The difference in our lives now was that when we went to work, Sonny came too. He fairly quickly overcame his carsickness, for which I was very grateful. It was no fun washing the dog van out at the end of every shift in what was a very cold January. I became immune to having frozen fingers and cold feet while sloshing about with a hosepipe in the back yard of the nick.

Because it was such a bad winter, we did not immediately put Sonny out into the kennel and he burst into our domestic bliss like an over-active tornado. It was almost unbelievable to see the amount of damage a young dog could do. Several chair legs, the bottom of the settee and the kitchen door all succumbed to Sonny's teething problems in the first few hectic months, but fortunately both sets of neighbours were elderly and somewhat hard of hearing, so they couldn't hear what I was shouting at him.

By the end of March we decided that the weather had eased enough for Sonny to be able to go into what had been Triton's kennel. Triton had lived in there quite happily all the time I had had him, but for the last year or so as he got older, we had him living in the house to help his old bones a bit. Sonny's first stay in the kennel lasted about 20 minutes.

I did all the right things. I put his blanket in the sleeping compartment. I gave him his favourite toy. I stayed with him in the wire netting run for ages playing with him and then eventually left him with encouraging words of praise.

A short while later I was reading the paper when a familiar head popped up over the outside window ledge, looking very pleased with itself. I went back down the garden with Sonny and surveyed the wreckage of the bottom half of the kennel door.

After suitable chastisement, out came the hammer and nails and bits of fresh wood until an appropriately reinforced door took shape.

I put Sonny back in the kennel and watched him from behind the greenhouse.

The crafty little devil must have known I was there, and sat as quiet as a mouse looking a picture of innocence as if butter wouldn't melt in his mouth. After half an hour of this I got bored with the whole thing and went back to the kennel and gave Sonny a bit of fuss and left him there.

Less than an hour later I was making a cup of tea, with Triton curled up comfortably in his corner in the kitchen, when there was a determined scratching at the back door. Triton pricked his ears towards the sound and then looked up at me, rolling his eyes as he did so. He got to his feet and padded out of the kitchen and into the living room. He knew what was coming and he was getting out of range.

I opened the kitchen door and grabbed Sonny by the scruff of the neck. Ignoring the squealing I dragged him back down the garden and once again contemplated the destruction he had wreaked. A homicidal maniac with a chainsaw could not have done much more damage to the door, it was now irreparable.

I gave Sonny a full-volume bollocking from a range of about six inches nose to nose, but quite unabashed he spoilt the whole thing by licking my nose before I had finished. I gave up and Sonny lived in the kitchen with Triton from then on. The kennel stood forlornly at the bottom of the garden and became the home of the lawnmower and other sundry garden tools.

Despite being almost constantly shouted at for some misdemeanour or other, Sonny continued to grow at an almost alarming rate.

From being short and fat with big feet, he grew to be long and thin with big feet. At 4 ½ months one of his ears managed to stick up into its correct, erect position, giving him a permanent, almost comic, quizzical look until the other one followed suit a couple of weeks later and he began to look more like a young Alsatian instead of a little furry pig.

Sonny's advance to maturity brought other problems in the camp. Triton had always enjoyed his food and usually managed to demolish the contents of his feeding bowl in the time it took me to scrub out and re-fill his water dish. But Sonny was really an expert in this field. He was absolutely voracious and simply attacked his food like there was to be no tomorrow.

I became quite adept at placing the three bowls of food (our old Bedlington terrier was the third of the trio) in three separate corners of the Kitchen in record time, fighting my way through waving tails, lolling tongues and excited brown eyes as I did so. All had gone well for a few months, but then, as he grew, Sonny got greedy.

One evening after he had scoffed his food, apparently in two enormous gulps, he decided to try for seconds and firmly stuck his nose into Triton's food. This was not the first mistake in his young life, but it was the biggest so far. Triton may have been old, but he wasn't soft. He seized Sonny round the back of the neck, shook him violently and in a split second there was a very exciting dog fight crashing round our rather small kitchen. Nimbus, the Bedlington, joined in enthusiastically. He may have looked a bit like a poodle, but he was all terrier at heart and he loved a good fight.

With much shouting and yelling by me and Ann and some judicious use of the broom, I broke it up and the participants all stood there panting, eyeing each other warily. Then Triton shook himself and with an almost contemptuous shrug of his still massive shoulders, turned his back on Sonny and resumed his interrupted lunch.

His whole being proclaimed to one and all, 'I'm still the boss and don't you forget it'. Sonny, much chastised, slunk away into a safe corner, ears flattened and with nervous eyes glancing anxiously behind him. He was learning the hard way.

But learn he did, and to be fair, Sonny was a very apt and willing pupil and it was not long before I was reliving the early days of Triton's training. With Sonny being so much younger than Triton was when I had him, to start with it was more a case of doing the right things preparatory to training, at least for the first few months. As a small example, I started by walking him to heel on my left-hand side.

All professional dog handlers, whether they be police, armed services or whatever, always walk their dogs on their left. Don't ask me why, it's probably something to do with carrying a sword, but on the left side it is, so it was 'left hand down a bit' for Sonny, and I was able to avoid the problems some handlers have when they take over an older dog.

If you've ever tried to convert a dog of, say, 12 months old who has habitually walked on the right-hand side of its previous owner, well let's just say 'it ain't easy folks'. It involves a lot of tripping over leads and falling over dogs and much shouting.

As the months went by, Sonny progressed well through all the basics of tracking, searching and biting, so well in fact, that by the time he was 12 months old he needed just a four-week course to finalize his training instead of the usual 13 weeks. It showed the advantages of 'running on' a young dog with an old dog. It seemed to give the youngster extra confidence having the big old fellah about and I'm sure Triton taught him some of the tricks of the trade.

On a Friday in October, Triton retired and, after a weekend off, on the Monday morning I took them both for an early morning walk before Sonny and I left for the Regional Dog Training School. I put Sonny straight into the back of my estate car and took Triton into the house when we returned.

I stroked his proud old head and made a fuss of him, but I tried to keep my departure deliberately low key for his sake (and mine). But you can't work together for ten years without knowing each other's minds and Triton knew exactly what was happening. Oh yes, he knew. As I drove off he sat broken-hearted by the front window, staring down the road, long after the car had gone, willing me to return. Ann comforted him, but he was inconsolable, and while we all know that dogs can't cry, Ann swore there were tears in his eyes.

The next day, and from then on, for the rest of his life, I took him with me, everywhere.

# CHAPTER TWENTY TWO

## *A SPECIAL PET*

After Sonny had successfully passed out from the Regional Training School as a proper police dog (complete with a certificate of competence, would you believe), I was faced with a problem.

I had been taking Triton with me while Sonny was training and he was quite happy to snooze away in the back of my estate car while I was busy with the youngster.

Occasionally I would run through an exercise with him so he could show these young upstarts how it should be done, and you could almost see him swelling with pride as he showed off his various abilities. It did the novice dog handlers no harm at all either, to feel a real dog bite through the arm guard and experience a bit of actual pain. The difference between a bite of an eleven year old as opposed to an eleven month old dog has to be felt to be believed and we saw some interesting facial expressions as Triton clamped his still powerful jaws round some unfortunate's wrist. It was all good clean fun.

But to return to the problem of what to do with Triton when I went back to my divisional duties. I couldn't leave him at home, it would break his heart; and I couldn't take him with me...or could I?

I decided that Trition's well being came before any other consideration and as I had been carting two dogs around for nine months anyway, while Triton was working and Sonny was being 'run on', I guessed correctly that nobody would notice. As it happened, Triton's presence came in very handy.

He had always been extremely popular at all the schools we visited and now if anything, he became more so, with all the school children adopting him as their special pet.

He was completely trustworthy with children and was quite happy to be fondled and patted by any number of kids at once. This helped to take a bit of the pressure off Sonny and allowed me to ease him into this aspect of his job more gradually than would have otherwise been the case.

After a few months, everyone became so used to seeing me with two dogs in tow it was regarded as being perfectly normal and there was never a raised eyebrow. Sonny did all the actual police work of course, and was soon notching up prisoners of his own, much to my delight.

There is almost nothing quite so rewarding as the feeling you get when your dog finds some little villain cunningly concealed in an apparently safe hidey-hole. Mind you, the thrill of the chase and the glow of a good capture is all one-sided, criminals definitely do not like police dogs, they tend to spoil their whole day. Quite right too. Somebody should, and Sonny, like Triton before him, was becoming just the dog to do it.

As the months flew by, Sonny started to thicken out and mature. His chest dropped and expanded, his neck became thick and muscular and he developed into a fine-looking dog, very reminiscent of Triton in his younger days. His temperament was the same too, as a rather spectacular arrest in front of most of the staff and pupils of a local comprehensive school was to prove.

I had gone there to give a talk to the somewhat rebellious fifth form. To be fair, the lecture had gone very well, plenty of laughs and absolutely no trouble, although I suppose with Triton and Sonny lying at my feet there was a great incentive on behalf of the listeners to pay rapt attention to the pearls of wisdom dropping from my lips. My dogs had a great way of dealing with any would-be hecklers.

As I was leaving, the headmaster intercepted me and asked if I could assist him remove half-a-dozen drunken ex-pupils who were causing a fair bit of havoc in the playground. I went to my van and after helping Triton climb in, I went to find out who was ruining the peace and tranquillity.

Knowing the area well, I had already made a fair guess as to who they might be, and my suspicions were confirmed as I turned the corner. I knew at least three of them were already well known to the police, and one of these was flagrantly relieving himself up one of the netball posts while shouting something about breaking the school record. His mates were encouraging him with an impressive array of obscenities. All this was in front of a mixed audience of 12, 13 and 14-year-olds.

'Enough', I shouted, 'You. Put that away and come here'.

Emboldened by the alcohol and the presence of his mates, he waved his willy towards me and shouted an uncomplimentary reply. I was not happy. He had had his chance. I went towards him.

'Right mate,' I said, 'You are nicked, come here.'

Realization dawned on him much too late that he had gone too far. He looked round wildly for an escape route and started to run. His five cronies contrived to block my way to him for a second or so, until Sonny cleared them rapidly out of the way leaving his target in full view.

I was having my doubts about using the dog for what is a relatively minor offence, but the young man made things a lot easier for me by launching a cider bottle in my direction as he ran. As the bottle smashed in front of me, I released Sonny.

It was his first real-life chase and bite and my heart was in my mouth as he hurtled after our drunk. Would he do it right first time? Especially in front of all these people. 'Yeah'. The cry involuntarily escaped from my mouth as Sonny launched himself into the air, bit hard into the young man's upper arm and brought him crashing to the ground. Sonny released his grip as I ran up to him, and I pulled out very shaken prisoner to his feet.

'All this for having a piss?' he protested.

'No son', I said, 'It's for taking the piss.'

I radioed for transport and after the now very subdued prisoner had been taken away by two of my colleagues, I took Sonny back to the dog van. Triton had heard all the commotion from inside his cage and had seen the final act of Sonny's arrest through the back windows. As I opened the doors Triton reached out and nuzzled Sonny's nose. I could almost hear him say, 'Well done young man, I couldn't have done better myself.' As usual, he was absolutely right.

Triton continued as our unofficial public liaison police dog for the next two years or so. As old dogs do, he got slower and slower and stiffer and stiffer, but still his eyes brightened when I put my uniform on. Still he whined with excitement in his cage when he heard the motor drive of the blue light going round on the roof. Still he could give a deep-throated bark as support to Sonny when he heard my voice raised at some troublemakers outside his van.

Still he followed me everywhere, until one morning, just short of his fourteenth birthday, when I came downstairs in uniform as usual, I knew instantly something was wrong. Sonny was there at the bottom of the stairs alright, but strangely subdued. Not bouncing up and down as normal. He turned away from me and looked significantly towards the back room.

Triton, where was Triton? I rushed in. Triton lay still on the hearthrug. I knelt by him and gently lifted his old head in my hands.

His breathing was so faint I could hardly feel it. At my touch his eyes opened briefly and looked into mine for what I knew would be the last time. Then they closed and he was gone - in death as in life, with absolute dignity.

# About the author

Steve Lewis joined Birmingham City Police as a raw recruit in 1965. After 4 years service he transferred to the Dog Section and, after the Force was amalgamated into the West Midlands Police, he was promoted to the rank of Sergeant in 1976, still working with his first beloved Police Dog Triton.

During 26 years as a Dog Handler, Steve was privileged to handle three dogs in all, with Sonny and Dusty following in Triton's illustrious paw prints.

Steve retired in 1995, after serving for 30 years as a Police Officer and now lives in Wales with his lovely wife Ann. Dusty was 9 years old at the time and lived on for another 5 years in happy retirement. Two Golden Retriever / Labrador Cross Breed, brother and sister, Mack and Mabel, (don't ask) followed, for a long time, and Steve and Ann now have a beautiful female German Shepherd whose name is Gena (and who is frighteningly intelligent).

You might just detect from the above, that all their dogs, although well trained, have also been much loved!

Printed in Great Britain
by Amazon

15258233R00059